Fred M. Wood

Hosea:

Prophet of Reconciliation

5132-16

This book is the text for course 3216 of Subject Area 32, Bible Studies, of the Church Study Course.
Target group: This book is designed for adults and is part of the Church Study Course offerings. The 1963 statement of "The Baptist Faith and Message" is the doctrinal guideline for the writer and editor.

Dewey Decimal classification number: 224.6
Printed in the United States of America

Contents

A Word to Begin With

Hosea is the name of a man who lived nearly 2,700 years ago. That we should even know he lived is remarkable. More remarkable, however, is the fact that through his experiences he came to a new understanding of God, an understanding which rose to the level of revelation. His writing is in our Bible because of that fact.

What was Hosea's revelation about God? That God's love does not stop with judgment, but moves through and beyond it to offer man redemption and reconciliation. Paul put Hosea's insight in this way: "Love never faileth" (1 Cor. 13:8, ASV [1]).

Our author, Dr. Fred M. Wood, presents Hosea's concept of God's love and man's reconciliation in a beautiful and tender manner. You may be acquainted already with this writer's warmth through his contributions to Adult Sunday School materials and his several Broadman Press books such as *Fire in My Bones*. This spiritual warmth and depth can be sensed also in *Hosea: Prophet of Reconciliation*.

The use of this book will occur in personal or group study. In either case, personal learning activities at the end of each chapter are included to help the user fix the learning that has taken place. When study is done in a group, the study leader will guide members in the appropriate use of this feature. Guidance for use of the learning activities in individual study will be found on pages 136-138.

Upon completion of this book study, the reader should return the application for credit form on page 139. Two copies of the credit award will be mailed to the applicant's church—one for the church's record, the other for individual use.

Ralph L. Murray
Editor

[1] In this book the Bible text used is the American Standard Version, unless otherwise stated.

1
A Tender Man in a Tangled World

HOSEA 1:1

How do we know the meaning of a prophet's message? We must know, first of all, the facts of his life. We must be aware of the times in which he lived. The pressures he faced and his unique personal problems must be studied. A prophet did more than tell the future; he dealt with the issues of his day. His first word was for his own people. Truth, however, is timeless. This fact means that his message applies to us even as it did to the people of the prophet's own day.

1. The Man God Sent

God sent more than a series of sermons to decaying and doomed Israel in the eighth century before Christ. He sent a man. God spoke to Hosea in many ways, and especially through his experiences. Hosea in turn spoke God's messages to Israel. We have those messages in the book that bears his name.

His Name

The Israelites were careful in giving names to their children. Names often stood for traits which the parents felt the child had, or would have in the days to come. Sometimes a name was tied up with the events present in the country when he was born. Jeremiah's parents named him "Jehovah hurls." He was born during the dark days of Manasseh's reign. They hoped God would use their son to "throw" a message to the nation and even to the king himself. Habakkuk wrestled with the age-long problem of why the righteous suffer. His name means "embracer," which describes his career well.

The word "Hosea" means "salvation" and is identical with the proper name Joshua. It is very close to the name of our Savior. Hosea's name fit his task well. He was the last prophet to Israel before she fell in 722 B.C. He pleaded for the people to turn to God and be saved. He may be called the prophet of the decline and fall of the Northern Kingdom. He sought to call the sinful and estranged nation back to God.

His Home and Family

Hosea is called "the son of Beeri" (1:1). This fact is all we know about his family. We find a Beerah (a Reubenite prince) in 1 Chronicles 5:6, but there is nothing to show this man was the prophet's father.

The prophet's references to farm life suggest a rural background. He may have tilled the soil in his youth. Yet he had knowledge of current events. His language is terse, but beautiful, and contains many figures of speech which only a cultured man would employ. Hosea may have been a member of the wealthy rural class.

That he was a native of the Northern Kingdom seems clear, his remarks to Judah seeming to be only side-glances. He loved the land that he said would be destroyed. One cannot help feeling that the prophet's heart came near to breaking when he beheld his fellow Israelites throwing themselves headlong into ruin. Amos spoke as though he were in the land on a visit. Hosea was one with the people. We cannot be sure what part of Israel was Hosea's home. Many students feel it was that strip of country—mountainous, yet fertile—between Bethel and Jerusalem. It overlooked the Jordan Valley.

What was his occupation? Two ideas have been set forth. First, some have felt he was a priest. He referred often to them and their work. He also felt free to condemn them sharply. He spoke of the "law" (4:6; 8:12) and referred to "unclean food" (9:3), to "the shameful thing" (9:10), and to the "house of his God" (9:8). Ezekiel spoke the same way, and we know he was a priest. Others believe Hosea was a baker. He describes the heated oven and the flaming fire (7:6-7). There are not enough facts to warrant our assertion of either vocation for Hosea.

His Personality

Both as a man and a prophet Hosea was a colorful person. As one who felt deeply, he gained his gospel through his grief. He was a poet with keen insight, though a man of contrasts. He could be the saddest and gladdest of men. The prophet could see heaven and hell at the same time. He could ride on the wings of an eagle, and then be dragged down to earth. He could flame up like a volcano, then soothe like a brook. Hosea saw the coming gloom, yet could see beyond the dark cloud to God's dawning light. He was the Jeremiah of the Northern Kingdom.

Hosea was frank, but refined, in his preaching, and never brought offense to the good taste of his hearers. The prophet was both a student of history and one who was keen in matters of daily life. Although we know nothing of his formal training, his use of the Hebrew proves he was far from dull.

Hosea and the Other Prophets

Amos had a very brief period of preaching in Israel. He most likely came a few years before Hosea. Amos may have spoken his word and gone back to Judah before Hosea came on the scene. Isaiah and Micah preached during the latter part of Hosea's life. Most students accept the following dates: Amos—760 B.C.; Isaiah—740 B.C.; and Micah—735 B.C. Hosea began preaching about 753 B.C. or a little sooner. That he kept on the job until the fall of the Northern Kingdom in 722 B.C. is likely.

The contrast between Amos and Hosea is great. Each preached a part of God's message. They did not contradict each other; they brought to the people two aspects of Israel's God. These two prophets were men of such great force that George Adam Smith in introducing Hosea spoke of "the problem that Amos left." [1] Amos was dark and austere. His message was direct. Hosea was as complex as Amos was simple. Hosea was tender, yet tough. Hope and grief dwelt side by side in his life and preaching. Did the two men know each other? Hosea may have heard the stern Amos preach one of his severe rebukes at Bethel. It may be that Amos spoke so harshly of the coming judgment that he offended the sensitive soul of Hosea. Possibly Hosea felt Amos' harsh message presented an unfair picture of God. Hosea thought of God as a loving Father grieving over his erring children.

His Concern with Political Affairs

Hosea did not mention any of Israel's rulers by name. He did not approve of them as leaders. His charges against Ephraim include veiled statements about the monarchs. His words about treaties with foreign nations reflect his disgust with every policy in royal circles. When we pass into chapters 4—14, we sense that the nation's leaders were falling quickly. Hosea spoke of Samaria's king as "cut off, as foam upon the water" (10:7). Just before this description, he pictured the people as saying, "We have no king; for we fear not Jehovah; and the king, what can he do for us?" (10:3). In a prior section Hosea charged that the people "devour their judges; all their kings are fallen" (7:7). Unlike Amos (Amos 7:10-17), Hosea was able to avoid a direct clash with the kings. He was not, as Isaiah, a close friend with his country's monarchs.

Hosea was a student of foreign affairs. He was aware that Israel had sought the help of Assyria. His statement in 5:13, no doubt, referred to tribute sent by Menahem to Tiglath-pileser in 738 B.C. Hosea also may have referred to Judah's part under Ahaz in the Syro-Ephraimitic War. He knew of Shalmaneser's victory over Beth-arbel (10:14). Hosea did not say much about his nearby neighbors, but neither did he ignore them nor think them worthless. Although he did not have Amos' worldwide outlook, he was far from a local yokel with a narrow viewpoint. Hosea was aware of trends in history. He related his preaching to them and to his nation's future.

His Call and Ministry

We cannot be certain about the relation of Hosea's marriage to the time of the prophet's first preaching. To say his call came only after Gomer broke his heart by leaving him is not right. There seems good reason to believe he was a prophet even before God told him to marry Gomer. He did gain deeper insight into God's purposes because of his tragic family life. R. E. Wolfe pictures the Tekoan hills at night as the setting of Amos' summons to preach. Wolfe believes Hosea came to know more of God's will for his life during his courtship with the young woman he had come to love. Wolfe contends Amos was "transformed in an instant," [2] but Hosea was changed over a period of time. Hosea's ideals and fervor were begun and nurtured during his courtship. His life was fulfilled in a larger way as he expressed himself in his public preaching.

Whether Hosea preached a short time like Amos or many years, we cannot be certain. He may have brought only two or three public discourses. Pusey [3] and Morgan [4] contend he preached at least seventy years. The book of Hosea says the prophet began preaching before the house of Jehu was destroyed (1:4) at the death of King Zechariah (2 Kings 15:8-12). The date was about 753 B.C. Hosea was active as late at least as the reign of Menahem in Israel. He referred to the payment of tribute by that king to Assyria (12:1); this event would place him as late as 738 B.C. Beyond this date we must only surmise. The latter part of Hosea's book reflects urgent crisis. We cannot escape the feeling that Hosea was still on the scene when the Northern Kingdom fell to Assyria in 722 B.C.

2. The World in Which Hosea Lived

To be alive in the eighth century before Christ meant danger. It also meant thrill and newness. That world, like our own, was on the move. Shocks came often because of rapid change in both leaders and events.

Political Overview

In Hosea's time the balance of power among the nations was shifting. Syria's strength of the previous century had been crushed; she was no longer a threat to Israel. Egypt was still mighty to promise, but midget to produce. Isaiah (30:7) called her "Rahab that sitteth still." She could never be ignored, but she posed no real problem at this time. Babylon's day had not yet come. It would be more than a hundred years before she became a factor in the power struggle among the nations. Neither of the two countries east of Jordan—Moab nor Ammon—was strong enough to cause any worry for Israel or Judah. Edom to the south was also not to compete. Assyria had been a strong nation, but was at this time in a dormant state.

In the second half of the eighth century Assyria rose quickly to power. She came on strong under four forceful kings: Tiglath-pileser (745-727 B.C.), Shalmaneser (727-722 B.C.), Sargon (722-705 B.C.), Sennacherib (705-681 B.C.). Within the span of these four kings Israel was destroyed, and Judah was brought to her knees.

The first three kings of Israel were Saul, David, and Solomon. At Solomon's death in 931 B.C. the kingdom was split into two nations. Ten tribes retained the name Israel. The other two became known as Judah.

Two strong kings came to Israel and Judah about the same time. Jeroboam II began in 794 B.C. He ruled Israel forty-one years. Uzziah began in 792 B.C. He ruled Judah fifty-two years. Both kings were left free from major wars. An intense feeling of pride arose in the nations. The border of the two countries was restored "from the entrance of Hamath to the sea of Arabah" (2 Kings 14:25). This period was a return to the balmy days of Solomon. The Old Testament says little about Jeroboam II, but he was one of Israel's strongest kings.

At Jeroboam's death the Northern Kingdom declined quickly. Six kings followed him in rapid order. Under them the nation fell apart. Only one of these last six rulers died a natural death. The other five were killed in cold blood. Israel's period of peace was gone.

In 745 B.C., Tiglath-pileser became king of Assyria. He had one goal: to include all the nations in his empire. The last six kings of Israel lived with this fact. They became either pro-Assyrian or pro-Egyptian, according to their bent. In 738 B.C., King Menahem of Israel made a crucial decision. He paid heavy tribute to Assyria, but the peace he bought was short-lived. He was succeeded by his son, Pekahiah, who was in turn killed by Pekah. Pekah turned to Egypt for help. Tiglath-pileser came to deal with the rebels. The land was ravished; many people were taken away; only Samaria and the hill country round about it remained free. Pekah was killed by Hoshea, who then took charge of Israel. He paid tribute to Assyria and made the nation a vassal. The wealth of the early years was lost in the vain effort to hold off the brutal armies of Assyria.

Wealth and Social Disorder

The peace brought by Jeroboam and Uzziah also brought wealth. More trade meant more profit. Nothing could halt the mad race for riches. The people enjoyed the luxury brought to them by their strong kings. Those who came after Jeroboam coasted on his momentum. The people's quest for wealth brought about a crucial problem. A widening gap began to appear between the economic classes. Within a few years the poor were reduced to the level of slaves. The stable middle class was gone. The wealthy controlled the land, and they managed things so as to bring gain to themselves. Israel's way of life became urban rather than rural. In the early days all the people lived on the land. As the landowners' wealth increased, they moved to the city. They wanted the safe, easy city life with all its comforts. The newly rich upper class enjoyed their summer and winter homes. They stayed apart from the common people, and were not concerned with the problems of the poor. The upper class wanted the nation to prosper, but ignored social sin and human need.

Some readers feel Hosea ignored social justice. This charge is not fair. On one occasion, he shouted, "There is nought but swearing and breaking faith, and killing, and stealing, and committing adultery; they break out, and blood toucheth blood" (4:2). Hosea was keenly aware that the weak suffer at the hands of the strong.

Religious Pluralism and Israel's Idolatry

Before the Israelites entered Canaan under Joshua, they had found something new. It was a religion based on a strong appeal to man's lustful nature and sex drive. The pagan Canaanites were many separate groups within the one designation, having different tribal names. Their type of worship became a strong rival to the Israelites' pure and simple worship. The Hebrews' earliest contact with this form of worship was at Baal-peor east of Jordan before they came into the Promised Land (Num. 25:3; 31:16; Deut. 4:3). Hosea (9:10) claimed Israel began to sin even before crossing the Jordan.

A few of this Canaanite system's chief features will give one a knowledge of the prophet's problem. The Canaanites served a number of gods. The chief one was Baal. He was linked with the land's fertility. His bitter foe was Moth, the god of summer drought and the lord of death. An ancient myth told how Moth fought Baal and killed him. The goddess Anath—called Ashtaroth in the Old Testament—avenged Baal's death. Baal then arose from the dead and was held to be the husband of the land. He related to the people in terms of sex. Women were kept on the staff in order to engage in sex with the worshipers. The man engaged in sex and then made a gift to Baal. The act and the gift were supposed to assure the farmer of fertile land. The people were acting out the part of the god's marriage with the land. The women so involved were not considered wicked in any sense. They were thought to be engaged in a decent and even godly career.

How did the Israelites feel about Baal worship? Moses had warned his people against having an easy conscience toward these pagans. In one of his last speeches to the Israelites he spoke sternly, "Ye shall surely destroy all the places wherein the nations . . . served their gods" (Deut. 12:2). Moses meant that in the high mountains, in the hills, and under all the green trees the Israelites were to break down the pagan altars and dash in the pillars. Jehovah's people were to burn the pagan gods with fire and hew down the graven images. In short, they were to rid the land of every shred of pagan religion. The Israelites were not obedient. Their ways may be described by the words of Alexander Pope, who in his *An Essay on Man* said,

> *Vice is a monster of so frightful mien*
> *As to be hated needs but to be seen;*
> *Yet seen too oft, familiar with her face,*
> *We first endure, then pity, then embrace.*[5]

Why did Israel not obey? Several answers may be given. The first is pluralism. The Israelites believed the two forms of worship could exist side by side. At first they were separated. Then the

Israelites began to use some of the Baal rites in their worship of Jehovah. The final step was a merging of the two. This process is called syncretism. When it happens, the stricter usually gives way to the more lenient; lower standards result. More of Baal rubbed off on those who worshiped Jehovah than the opposite.

To trace Baal worship in the Northern Kingdom is not easy. It began at the death of Solomon. Jeroboam I had led the Northern Kingdom to worship God under the symbol of a golden calf. When Ahab and Jezebel came to be king and queen of the nation, a second step was taken. Worship of Baal took place without any restraint. Jezebel was a heathen princess. Her father was a priest who made himself king through murder. Jezebel led her husband to set up Baal worship as the established religion of Israel. Jehu, a later king, stamped it out as the state religion, but did not destroy it. Perverted worship had made its way into the life of the nation and remained until the bitter end.

During Hosea's day the pagan high places were present throughout the land. There was no restraint of man's lower nature. The morbid fears of guilt were erased by his offering. He sought to swap the fruit of his body for the sin of his soul. At the same time he satisfied every urge of his lower nature.

The people did not intend, even in Hosea's day, to forsake Jehovah as they worshiped Baal. They felt their ancient God could meet some of their needs, but Baal supplied others. In defense of the country they called upon Jehovah of Hosts. In matters of food, water, clothing, oil, silver, and gold, Baal met their need. Israel had merged the worship of Baal and Jehovah so that she had two religions in one.

Moral Corruption

Israel's downward plunge began with her Baal worship. By the time of Hosea the full bitter fruits had come. The stream became darker as it flowed into unbridled lust. By Hosea's day, worship had become nothing but a sex orgy (4:12-14). Pusey has written of Israel's worship: "Corruption had spread throughout the whole land; even the places once sacred . . . Bethel, Gilgal, Mizpah, Shechem, were especial scenes of corruption or of sin. Every holy memory was effaced by present corruption. Could things be worse?" [6]

This type of abuse led to other sins. People who indulge in fleshly excess seldom make up for it by noble conduct in other parts of their lives. The people were equally wicked in dealing with their weaker brothers. Injustice prevailed; fraud was rampant. Courts were corrupt because the judges were smitten with love of money. The prophet spoke often concerning bribes. Judges, for even a small gift, took the side of the rich against the poor. Large estates were built in a short time by buying off the judges and taking the holdings of the poor. There was no feeling of guilt for such action. The deprived man was reduced to the status of a slave and was then sold into bondage for a small price.

The women were no better than the men. In many cases they were worse. The women urged their husbands to be greedy and unjust so that the family income would be increased. The wealth gained was used to satisfy the whims of the women. The kingdom was crumbling. Hosea saw clearly that the moral standards in the land were causing a decay which would make Israel an easy prey to an outside army.

Spiritual Blindness

How could things get into such foul shape? The answer is that Israel forgot the true nature of her God. She failed to keep in mind God's purpose when he chose her as his own. God did not desire merely to set a people apart for their own glory; he had chosen them to reveal himself to the world. Israel had come to think that God would be her ally always, even when she ignored his command for righteous living.

Moses, however, had warned Israel before she received the law at Sinai: "Ye have seen what I did unto the Egyptians, and how I bare you on eagles' wings, and brought you unto myself. Now therefore, if ye will obey my voice indeed, and keep my covenant, then ye shall be mine own . . . and ye shall be unto me as a kingdom of priests, and a holy nation" (Ex. 19:4-6). False worship and immoral deeds create a vicious circle. False worship leads to a decline in moral standards because we become like that which we worship. If our god has no moral nature, there is no urge toward holy living. Our depraved conduct is confirmed by our false god. Bad deeds and false worship each feed the other.

Israel's worship caused her way of life to become both wicked and empty. Spiritual blindness came upon the people. Hosea stated it clearly, "Whoredom and wine and new wine take away the understanding" (4:11). Israel became captive to her own false worship. She came to lack insight and was unable to know right from wrong.

Prophetic Direction

The prophet spoke for God. He brought a living word to the people of his own day. He spoke often concerning the future. His message, though, was based on the fact of God's living presence in the moral law of the world he created. God's will was related to his redemptive program and always was guided by it.

The prophet was more than a spokesman. The Hebrew word used more often for "prophet" in the Old Testament comes from a root which means "to speak." The spoken word was urgent, but the prophet's life spoke more forcefully.

The prophet was a man who felt deeply that God had placed a burden upon his soul. He was austere, but he was also tender. His words were often stern, sharp, and stinging, but behind his words was the deep conviction that God's love would win the victory. He believed there was a bright future for his people. Almost all the prophets began with a message of doom, but sooner or later made their way to a message of hope.

People of every age need wise guidance. Sinful man and holy God meet in the statements of the Hebrew prophets, who realized the time was late in Israel's history. The nation was rushing to chaos; someone had to call the people back. Although the prophet often seemed harsh, he had a good reason: his nation's future depended upon his arousing the people. They had to know how serious things were. All the people were not equally guilty, but all had to be called to share in the task of helping the nation back. The prophet had to speak his message, even though it brought offense to those who heard. He was to do his duty as God laid it upon his heart. Whether the people heard or refused to hear, they would know a prophet had been in their midst.

Since the days of Israel, mankind had produced nothing that can be compared with the Hebrew prophets. They were one of the greatest forces for good the world has ever seen. Jesus of Nazareth linked himself to Israel's prophets. He was the purest blossom and fairest flower of the noble movement. Jesus was more than a prophet, however. He was God's perfect Word clothed in frail human flesh.

3. A Look at His Book

Although we do not know how long Hosea preached, we do have the substance of his earnest appeals. His messages are written in the book which bears his name. We can depend on the book's being what it claims to be—a message directly from Hosea.

A *Difficult Book*

How does the average reader know Hosea? Mostly through verses picked at random as proof texts to emphasize a particular truth. The book is not a usual one and is easy neither to read nor study.

There are reasons for its being hard to grasp. Local color, often vague and obscure, is found frequently in the book. Much of the book seems to be made up of excerpts from oral addresses which cover a long period of time. One verse may picture doom while the next promises better days. How can we explain these quick shifts? The book comes from a sensitive man who suffered greatly. A comparison of the book to the writings of a soldier at the front in the thick of battle is warranted. The fetters of grammar do not suffice for Hosea's deep feeling. The images and thoughts push and pursue one another. Torn with agony and tragic times, Hosea is one of the saddest books in the Old Testament. It could have been titled "The Lamentations of Jehovah." Still, it is one of the greatest books in the Bible. If we will dig deeply into its contents, we will find profound truths to enrich our lives.

A Genuinely Delightful Book

Before Hosea preached, fear was the major motive which moved men to worship. God was a person of supreme power. To worship him meant to obey him without question. Hosea taught men that the essence of true religion is to know God as a person. Hosea looked inward for his knowledge of God. This truth, once taught by Hosea, was never again absent among the best thinkers of Israel. Amos pictured God as stern, but Hosea proclaimed him as one who suffered long because of his love. Jeremiah built on this concept, but Hosea first preached it. George Adam Smith contended that there is no truth spoken about divine grace by later prophets which is not found in Hosea.[7] The prophet spoke from a heart deeply moved and torn by grief. This agony gives the book a special charm. Another fact which speaks highly for the book is that it is quoted by New Testament writers more times (thirty) than any other of the minor prophets.

Hosea could be considered a failure. His nation did not turn to God and avoid judgment. On the other hand, his sermons still live to bless and change the lives of people. Among those who were moved by his burning words was a young boy who lived in Anathoth more than a hundred years after Hosea. That boy—Jeremiah—found in Hosea not only a teacher, but a soul kindred to his own. When we absorb Hosea's words and message, we too can know afresh the love of God as a tender in-depth force. Hosea made a last appeal to a nation that had sinned against her God and seemed beyond repentance. She seemed to have lost the desire to survive. Although Hosea lived long ago, his words speak forcefully to the moral and spiritual needs of our nation today. He meets the longing of each human spirit. Only Jesus surpasses him; few, if any, among the Old Testament prophets were Hosea's equal.

Analysis of Contents

The book has two sections, each of which is distinct in plan. Since the sections are not equal in length, some Bible students think the two sections may have been different books at one time. Later, after Hosea's death, they may have been combined into one book by one of his students.

The first section (chaps. 1—3) tells of the prophet's tragic homelife. His marriage and the birth of his children are told in 1:2-9. Gomer's sin is clearly indicated. The last two verses of chapter 1 contain a promise to Israel about her future. It is tied in through symbols to the children of Hosea. This promise is carried on through the first verse of chapter 2.

The third chapter records how the prophet went after his wayward wife. She seems to have been on the market as a slave. He bought her from the shame to which she had fallen, and restored her as his wife after a time of testing. The chapter concludes with a promise to Israel. She too must spend time in shame, but, like the prophet's wife, also will be restored.

In between these two sections is a poem (2:2-23) about Israel and Jehovah. By symbols it is woven into the life of Hosea and his wife, Gomer. It pictures God as a loving husband who cares for the nation. He will woo her back to be his loving bride again.

Chapters 4—14 are difficult to outline. No clear and concise outline is apparent. The passage appears to be a series of fragments concerning Hosea's life during the chaos before Israel's fall. The book is inspired by God, though, and meaning abounds in it for us. Four main divisions stand out.

The first division (4:1 to 6:3) contains a two-fold charge against the nation. The rebukes overlap. The first word is to the people; in 5:1 the leaders are singled out for reproach. The last three verses of the division (6:1-3) invite the people to return to the Lord. This section was, no doubt, one discourse. It was brought by the prophet during the early part of his ministry, shortly before or after the death of Jeroboam II.

The second section (6:4 to 10:15) contains a group of poems telling of the rapid decay in Israel. It may be they were brought as one sermon, but not likely. These poems represent the essence of Hosea's preaching near the end of the nation's history. The people are told to repent (10:12). The renewed threat of judgment which follows seems to say that Hosea did not expect them to heed the message.

The third section (11:1-11) is a poem concerning God's love for Israel. It matches the poem in 2:2-23 and pictures God as a loving father. It is perhaps the greatest single section in the book.

The last section (11:12 to 14:9) is a final word to the nation. At the end of the discourse there is love's final call as given by the prophet. This call concludes not only the sermon, but also serves as a fitting end for Hosea's entire message.

Hosea was a tender man who sought to live for God in tangled times. His life and God's dealings with him will be the basis of our further study.

---

[1] George Adam Smith, *The Book of the Twelve Prophets*, Vol. 1 (Garden City: Doubleday, Doran & Company, Inc., 1929), p. 236.

[2] Rolland Emerson Wolfe, *Meet Amos and Hosea* (New York: Harper and Brothers, 1945), p. 74.

[3] E. B. Pusey, *The Minor Prophets* (Grand Rapids, Michigan: Baker Book House, 1953), p. 10.

[4] G. Campbell Morgan, *Hosea: The Heart and Holiness of God* (New York: Fleming H. Revell Company, 1934), p. 7.

[5] Alexander Pope, *An Essay on Man*, in *The Book of Classic English Poetry*, selected by Edwin Markham (New York: Wm. H. Wise & Co., 1934), p. 1205.

[6] Pusey, *op. cit.*, p. 12.

[7] Smith, *op. cit.*, p. 239.

PERSONAL LEARNING ACTIVITIES

1. Match the following items:

____(1) Hosea	a. Contemporary to Hosea
____(2) Fall of the Northern Kingdom	b. Name means "salvation"
____(3) Amos	c. Israel's conqueror
____(4) Assyria	d. 722 B.C.
____(5) King Menahem	e. Last king of reference in Hosea

2. What was the idolatrous worship which brought Israel to judgment?

Answers:
1. (1) *b*, (2) *d*, (3) *a*, (4) *c*, (5) *e*; 2. Baal worship.

2
When Life Falls In

HOSEA 1:2-9

In the early years of marriage Hosea knew the kind of joy that comes only in a happy home. As time went on, though, shadows of doubt began to arise. At last, the things he suspected about his wife proved true. The roof fell in upon him, bringing an agony that no man knows unless he has walked with such grief.

1. A Strange Command for a Man of God (*1:2*)

When did God first speak his message to and through Hosea? Almost all English versions of the Bible translate verse 2 so that a connection appears between God's word to Hosea and his marriage to Gomer. Does that verse mean that God said nothing at all to Hosea until this time? Or does it mean that Hosea first came to know the true nature of God's message through his married life?

Few passages have been given so many meanings by interpreters. We must not attempt to make the matter too simple. Although the passage is difficult to translate, the truth is clear. Hosea learned his deepest lesson through his life with Gomer. Perhaps he began prophesying with more zeal than depth. Years later he looked back and wrote of this period. He was amazed at what he had learned about God through his marriage and homelife.

Many Christians today have had similar experiences. We often marvel that we were so shallow in our early lives. "How could I have known so little?" we ask at a fuller stage in life's growth. We should rejoice. It is a mark of God's grace that he uses people at all periods of life.

Was Gomer already an impure woman when she married? Many ideas have been set forth. One view holds that Gomer was wanton before her marriage. She even had children from this life, according to this view. Other Bible students say the whole story is either a vision or an allegory with no basis in fact.

The story, however, seems too real to be denied. Surely it is more than a vision. God sometimes spoke to men in visions. (See Ezek. 1:1; Isa. 6:1-6.) Hosea's experience, though, smacks too much of the real thing. His life was changed by it. All his ministry was touched by his relationship with Gomer. To make the account merely a vision or a symbol does not fit in with the facts.

The phrase "wife of whoredoms" (v. 2, KJV) or "wife of harlotry" (v. 2, RSV) is a Hebrew plural. The phrase means the woman was bent toward loose sex. The NEB says "take a wanton for your wife," [1] and this renders the Hebrew well. Gomer must have been from the background of the Baal cult worship. Her own mother may have been a priestess for a short time. For girls to serve in this role a few years and then be dismissed by the priest was quite common. She would then be allowed to marry and rear her own family.

The phrase "children of whoredoms" (v. 2, KJV) should not be pressed to mean that Gomer already had a family. As the story moves on, it seems clear Gomer came to the marriage without any children. The Lord was saying that any offspring of Gomer would have traits like the mother.

2. The Prophet's Marriage to Gomer (*1:3*)

Many Bible students have sought a symbol in the name Gomer, but none that pleases them all has been found. Some of the meanings set forth have been "completion," "the perfect one," and "fulfillment" (the last refers to punishment).

The phrase "daughter of Diblaim" probably refers to Gomer's father. Some interpreters have suggested that the phrase names the town or village from which she came. This suggestion is doubtful. No such locale has been found in Israel. That the writer would refer to Diblathaim in Moab (Num. 33:47) is unlikely. An attempt to make the word *Diblaim* refer in symbol to cakes of pressed figs has been made. Thus Gomer would be connected with idol worship and its supposed delights. George Adam Smith rejects this idea, calling it farfetched.[2] The best approach is to see this phrase as based on fact, with no symbolic meaning.

3. Hosea's Family and Israel's Doom (*1:3-9*)

Tragic grief came to Hosea's homelife. The author is delicate in telling the story, but the sorrow may be traced in the birth of his children. The name of each child was linked symbolically to Israel's coming doom.

Jezreel: Judgment Is Sure (*1:3-5*)

The name *Jezreel,* given to Hosea's first child, had a profound message. Its spiritual meaning was based on historical fact. In order to know that meaning, we should review the account in 2 Kings 9:1 to 10:31.

Ahab and Jezebel had zeal—but not the holy kind. Under them, Israel became filled with Baal worship. This corrupt foreign cult was given full support by royalty. When Ahab's grandson, Jehoram, came to Israel's throne, Ahaziah, another of Ahab's grandsons (through a daughter), ruled in Judah. Both nations then became so wicked that drastic action had to be taken.

Elisha the prophet anointed Jehu to be king over Israel. When Jehu began to reign, he showed great zeal. He quickly killed the kings of both Israel and Judah. He also slew all who were in any way heirs to the throne of Israel. In addition, hundreds, perhaps thousands, who worshiped Baal were put to death. On the surface, Jehu seemed to be doing the will of God. He was stamping out Baal worship. But as time went on, he, like most zealots, overdid the job. He became merely a bloody man. He failed to lead the people back to God. (In fact, under him the people went back to the kind of worship Jeroboam I had brought to Israel. This was the worship of Jehovah under the symbol of a golden calf, and was not the Baal worship espoused by Ahab and Jezebel.) Jehu, however, broke the powers of Baal in Israel for his time. Because of Jehu's zeal against Baal, God made him a promise. His sons until the fourth generation would sit on the throne of Israel. When Hosea came to the scene, Jehu's third descendant was king. Jehu's family tree was as follows: Jehu, Jehoahaz, Joash, Jeroboam II. Zechariah, Jehu's fourth descendant, had yet to reign before God's promise to Jehu would be fulfilled completely.

In addition to that royal history, the historic events which took place in Jezreel gave added meaning to Hosea's name for this firstborn son. Jezreel was the name of both a city and a famous valley. The valley runs from Mount Carmel near the Mediterranean Sea to the Jordan River. The town of Jezreel is at the southern edge of the valley on the northwest spur of Mount Gilboa. Today a village named Zerin is located there.

In the Valley of Jezreel, Ahab's queen had slain the good man Naboth in order to seize his vineyard. Here Jehu's zeal had brought about the famous bloodbath in which two kings and all the seeming heirs to Israel's throne had been killed ruthlessly.

Hosea wanted to teach Israel through the name he gave his first-born son. Therefore he chose the historic name Jezreel. Hosea under God's direction used the name Jezreel to warn Israel of coming judgment.

There is, of course, a two-fold sense of the coming judgment in this passage. First, Jehu's house would be removed. Hosea said, "Yet a little while, and I will avenge the blood of Jezreel upon the house of Jehu" (1:4). Most likely, Hosea made this statement while Jeroboam II was still on the throne. His son, Zechariah, the last member of the dynasty, ruled only six months.

A second word from the prophet is part of verse 4: The Lord would "cause the kingdom of the house of Israel to cease" (1:4). That the two prophecies were closely related is clear. Hosea was not wrong. The Northern Kingdom did exist only a brief time beyond the death of Zechariah.

In verse 5 the prophet pictured God as saying he would "break the bow of Israel in the valley of Jezreel." This was the most fitting place for Israel to meet judgment. Hosea's word came to pass in a unique way. The Greek version (Septuagint) of 2 Kings 15:10 tells how Zechariah was killed at Ibleam, which is in the Valley of Jezreel. The word "bow" is a symbol of power in the Old Testament (Gen. 49:24; Job 29:20; Jer. 49:35). Likely, Israel's strength was broken before 722 B.C., when her capital, Samaria, fell. Battles in and near Jezreel broke Israel's strength. Hosea 10:14 refers to Shalmaneser's spoiling of Beth-arbel, a city archaeologists have located east of the Jordan. If that is the correct site, then Beth-arbel's spoiling signaled Israel's fall. The normal approach to Samaria would have been across the Jordan and through the Valley of Jezreel. This was the place of Israel's chief wealth, and the best field for the Assyrian horses. In that plain also is another site, called Arbella, which could have been the site of Hosea 10:14. We do not know the exact place of the crucial battle fought before the final siege of Samaria. There is strong reason, though, to believe Hoshea, Israel's last king, made his final stand in this valley. Certain is the fact that Hosea's words were fulfilled. When Jezreel fell, the nation's fall was only a matter of time.

Lo-ruhamah: No Father's Pity (1:6)

The style becomes terse with verse 6. Only a few words were used by the writer to tell of the birth of the second child. Verse 6 repeats the form of verse 4 in order that the focus may be upon the child's name. The word "God" (KJV), "Jehovah" (ASV), "Lord" (RSV) is not in the Hebrew text. Also the text says "bare a daughter," rather than "bare him a daughter," and thus departs from the earlier literary form (v. 3). Many interpreters suggest that the writer was pointing out that even at this time Gomer had broken the marriage vows. This inference could be true, but we cannot be sure. Gomer's possible faithlessness also could be seen from the name given to the daughter—*Lo-ruhamah.*

The daughter's name comes from putting a prefix on a Hebrew word. The prefix can be translated "no" or "not," and negates the basic meaning of the word to which it is added. Brought over into the English, the prefix reads *lo* (see vv. 6,8, RSV, ASV, NEB). The basic word is handled the same way. The Hebrew word is simply made into an English word. The result is *ruhamah.* Thus translated, the daughter's name becomes *Lo-ruhamah.* Other translators render the meaning of the Hebrew word and its prefix in English. They come up with such names as "Not pitied" (RSV) and even "Uncompassionate." In the New Testament, Paul spoke of "not beloved" (Rom. 9:25), and Peter referred to "not obtained mercy" (1 Pet. 2:10). Both phrases are based on this passage in Hosea.

We cannot know all that is implied in the name nor by whom the child was fathered. When we apply the name to the nation, however, the message is clear. The daughter's name conveys the fact that God's mercy was being withdrawn from Israel. The nation's time was running out. The Northern Kingdom would be dissolved as a nation. The daughter's name does not explain why the kingdom was destroyed. Rather, it is a signpost to the fact that judgment was sure.

The Hebrew word upon which the daughter's name is based means more than "feeling sorry for" or even "having compassion." Some translators feel the word is derived from a root which produces the noun "womb." If this meaning is true, the verb stands for the way a parent relates to a child, or a brother to a brother. In other words, it is a filial term showing the tender love of family life. The word carries the idea of the strong aiding the weak. It also conveys the stirring of inner love as one feels his need for his fellowman. We often relate to each other in dependence. All these ideas are present in this striking Hebrew word which forms a part of the daughter's name. We should not forget that the word "not" or "no" is also part of her name.

The daughter's name hinted at a family scandal; it suggests a father who questions his relationship to his child. Whatever the dark family facts involved, the daughter's name was symbolic. Hosea used it as the launching pad for a word from God to the people. As the prophet's message was sent abroad throughout the land, the people received the truth. The nation Israel was left without mercy before her God. No longer would God show to Israel the kind of love a father extends to his children. The nation had broken with God. He was now within his right to withdraw his feeling as father. He had endured their follies and failures thus far, but the cup was full. The divine verdict was that judgment must fall upon Israel. In the name of the first child Hosea had said that one particular royal house must pass away. In God's name Hosea had tolled the knell for the nation. The second child's name affirmed that no way to turn back the certain doom of Israel remained.

Some translators do not accept the phrase "but I will utterly take them away" (v. 6, KJV) as the proper way to render the Hebrew. In its place they translate, "that I should in any wise pardon them" (ASV); "to forgive them at all" (RSV); "never again forgive them" (NEB); and "that I should in any way pardon them" (*The Amplified Bible* [3]). These varied renditions are not efforts to soften Hosea's decree of Israel's doom. The Hebrew words of verse 6 translate either way. Other passages in the book make clear that the nation would be punished. The newer versions seem more in line with the context, however. Hosea was dealing with the subject of forgiveness here. His thought was that Israel *by her own sin* had sealed her own doom. She had moved herself beyond the realm of forgiveness.

A Side Glance at Judah—A Word of Comfort (1:7)

As Hosea viewed the moral climate of the two countries, he realized that Israel had gone much further into sin than Judah. The Northern Kingdom had been rebellious from the start. The people had gone from bad to worse. Not one good king had sat upon Israel's throne. Judah, on the other hand, had at certain times shown deep insight into God's purpose for the nation. Some of her kings had been wicked, but others had been righteous. Hosea did not state it, but one fact must have played a part: A direct heir of David still sat upon the throne of Judah. God was simply not yet ready to allow a foreign power to capture Judah. Her captivity would come later, but not in Hosea's day.

Hosea may have alluded in verse 7 to God's rescue of Judah during the Assyrian crisis. In 701 B.C. the Assyrian Sennacherib circled Jerusalem. He demanded that it submit to him at once (2 Kings 18:1 to 19:35; Isa. 36:1 to 37:36). Jerusalem's future seemed almost hopeless. Hezekiah, the king, was on the verge of panic. He sought help from God's prophet, Isaiah. The Bible tells how God came to the king's aid. One hundred eighty-five thousand Assyrian soldiers died in their own camp.

Hosea made quite clear in verse 7 that Judah's help and triumph would not come through human efforts. She was required to trust the Lord with all her heart. She had to believe that God is willing and able to meet the need of every crisis. Deliverance would not come through Judah's abilities or skills, but through God's divine act in history. Nor would Judah be delivered because she was good. That she was better than Israel was true. God would act for her, however, because his grace is limitless. Through her, he was working out his purpose to redeem the world.

Lo-ammi: Not Mine (*1:8-9*)

Hosea described the third child's birth much as he had the second child's. Gomer bore *a* son—not bore *him* a son (v. 8). We cannot deny that Hosea was the father of this child merely because a pronoun is absent. On the other hand, the name does seem to speak a message. Hosea called him *Lo-ammi,* which means "not my people," or, as some have rendered it, "none of mine." The name strongly implies that Hosea knew the truth about Gomer: She was a faithless wife. By naming the third child *Lo-ammi* Hosea made his private truth public.

As Gomer had refused to honor Hosea, so Israel had refused to honor God. The basic reason for Israel's existence as a nation was thwarted. The country's doom was sealed. The name of the child would be a walking word from God. It would say that God had refused Israel as his own people.

Hosea's Grief and Israel's

Each of these three messages to Israel through the children's names speaks for itself. Yet they need to be seen as a unit. Each of the names is a sign which tells of a firm and hard decree. There was no way to avoid that which God had said would come to pass. Any of the three would have been enough to have warned the people that the nation's doom was sealed.

On the other hand, there is progress from child to child as the prophet moved forward in his messages. Each stage speaks of coming judgment; each stage grows more intense. With the birth of each child, Hosea seems to have become more certain of Israel's fate. His prophetic signs became clearer, and there was no mistaking his meaning.

Hosea's family life fell apart; the relationship between him and Gomer was broken off. The record does not tell us the exact time. Most likely, she departed shortly after the birth of the third child. In that broken relationship Hosea saw mirrored Israel's broken relationship with God. His family life was a parable of Israel's spiritual condition.

One other word needs to be said at this point: The Lord's word of judgment, once pronounced, is final except for one possibility. Should the wrongdoer repent, God will forgive. We should never forget, however, one fundamental truth about the Hebrew prophet and his message. Always, whether stated or not, a chance for the people to turn back to God was assured. Sometimes the prophet made this fact clear. Even when he did not say so, he still wanted to see them mend their ways and be saved.

Sometimes man seems to have made himself incapable of changing his ways. This is man's problem, not God's. God is ready to accept any sinner who will come to him with a contrite heart. Never is it too late for a guilty person to find help. God will forgive even at two seconds before the midnight hour. Of course, in order to secure God's pardon, true sorrow for sin must be expressed, not mere remorse. There is a difference. We must be sorry for our sins, not sorry that we have been caught in our sinning.

4. Lessons for Life from the Scriptures

Hosea lived nearly twenty-seven centuries ago. This fact does not mean his message is out of date. God speaks to us through the prophet's words. Years have not dimmed his message nor made it less true for the day in which we live.

A person's homelife is important. Home is the holy of holies for the family. If each member is happy and secure, the family is blessed. Each can face the world as a stable person, meeting problems with courage and coping power. Robert Rainey, a great churchman of nearly a hundred years ago, once was asked the searching question, "How do you endure it when men oppose you and even make fun of what you say?"

He replied, " 'I'm very happy at home!' " [4]

When a nation rejects God, it is doomed. To repeal or avoid the law, "the wages of sin is death" (Rom. 6:23), is impossible. Sin brings death to the body, death to ideals and goals, and the second death in the world to come. This law also applies to a nation. The true greatness of countries is found in those things which make its citizens great. Daniel Webster said, "If we abide by the principles taught in the Bible our country will go on prospering and to prosper, but if we and our posterity neglect its instructions and authority, no man can tell how sudden a catastrophe may overwhelm us and bury our glory in profound obscurity." [5]

Because God is holy, sin must be punished. The prophet spoke often of God's decree that he would punish sin. There is an even more vital truth involved. God not only *will* punish sin; God *must* punish sin. His world is structured in such a way that right will win and wrong will lose. If the wages of sin were not death, we all would be in trouble. There would be a hopeless flaw in the makeup of God's world.

Sin may affect those who come in the future. Each person must pay for his own sin. No one can avoid his own guilt. A companion truth may be stated thus: Sin's effects often go beyond the sinner. One who indulges in wicked living can transmit a defect to an offspring. A family can lack the good things of life because a father spends in wrong living the money needed at home. Likewise one generation can sin and cause the next one to suffer. Ahab, for instance, set in motion laws that could not be stopped. He brought on a large scale wrong concepts of worship to Israel. The land never fully came back to where it was before he and Jezebel lived. Sin is an awful thing. We must deal with it in a drastic manner, both as individuals and as a nation.

God will not leave us without comfort. To suffer is a part of life. We cannot avoid it. There is another truth which brings comfort: God's grace is always able to help us triumph over suffering. From the tragic times in life we learn lessons that can be learned in no other way. Tough times are often the prelude to conquest; after the conquest comes unbounded joy. God is with us. Who can be against us (Rom. 8:31)?

---

[1] From *The New English Bible*. Copyright © The Delegates of the Oxford University Press, and the Syndics of the Cambridge University Press, 1961, 1970. Reprinted by permission, as are all other quotations from this version. Each quote from this version will be indicated by NEB in parenthesis.

[2] Smith, *op. cit.*, p. 244.

[3] From *The Amplified Bible*. Copyright © Zondervan Publishing House, 1965. Used by permission, as are all other quotations from this version.

[4] Charles L. Wallis, ed., *A Treasury of Sermon Illustrations* (Nashville: Abingdon Press, 1950), p. 166.

[5] Walter B. Knight, *Three Thousand Illustrations for Christian Service* (Grand Rapids: Wm. B. Eerdmans Publishing Company, 1947), p. 43.

PERSONAL LEARNING ACTIVITIES

1. Use numbers 1-3 to place the names of Hosea's children in the order of their birth: ____ Lo-ammi, ____ Lo-ruhamah, ____ Jezreel.
2. The author suggests (check the correct statement):
   ____ (1) Gomer was impure when she married Hosea.
   ____ (2) Gomer had children out of wedlock before she and Hosea were married.
   ____ (3) Gomer was pure at the time of her marriage, but she had a bent toward wanton living because of the influence of Baal worship on her life.

Answers:
1. 3,2,1; 2. (3).

3

Love That Will Not Let Go[1]

HOSEA 2:2-23

God's everlasting love for Israel is presented as a poem. This love is so strong it will never die. Using symbols and allegory, the prophet made God's love graphic. The husband stands for God. The wife plays the role of Israel. The mother's lovers are the Baal images of Canaan. The children are urged to plead with their mother to cease from her wrongdoing.

As the discourse moves along, Hosea moves back and forth between his wife and the nation. Both have been untrue to their husbands. The prophet's language thus sometimes fits one and then the other. The background of the early verses includes the legal way for bringing charges against a wife who has gone astray. First, she is accused. Then the form of punishment is outlined.

Hosea wasted no time with sweet and sticky words. He described matters as they were. He told the nation she must be punished severely because of her sin. Yet triumph would be her future lot. Hosea knew God would redeem the people and bring them back to himself in years to come, but he also knew the nation first must face tragic days. Israel had lost her soul in trying to gain the pleasures the Canaanite world had to offer. Only after she had suffered would her life be made anew. Then she could fit into God's purpose for her. Israel deserved to suffer, but God refused to give her up. Israel's guilt was great, but God's grace was greater. He had chosen to reveal himself through her to the world. In this way he planned to bring salvation to all men. This plan might be delayed because of her sin, but it could not be defeated. God is always the Loving Seeker; he freely forgives and delights to show mercy.

1. A Charge Against the Wayward Bride (2:2-5)

The passage opens with commands directed to the children. The situation is urgent, a fact shown by the prophet's double use of the verb "contend" (v. 2). In symbol the command was intended for those Israelites who were still faithful. They were to plead with others in the land concerning the moral need. In the larger sense all of Israel belonged to God's family. Yet there was always an Israel within Israel—a remnant who had remained faithful to God. No matter how wicked the nation became, this nucleus was always present.

This section's format is pitched against the background of a law court. The expression "plead" or "contend" is a legal term. It is used often in the Old Testament for the Lord's quarrel with Israel. Sometimes it denotes mere human disputes and complaints. The clauses "she is not my wife, neither am I her husband" (v. 2) may have been based upon an old divorce custom of the Akkadians. Among some ancient people one could divorce his wife simply by making a formal statement. Such a statement was final with no appeal for it. We must not forget that in Hosea's message it was not God's plan to dismiss Israel. Instead, God longed to see her repent and come to her senses and to him. The children were urged to do all they could to persuade her to act wisely.

What would happen should Israel refuse to repent? She would be put to shame in public. Among many nations it was the custom to strip naked any woman who was guilty of adultery. There is no record of this practice among the Hebrews then. Some ancient Hebrew scribes said Leviticus 20:10 and Deuteronomy 22:22 mean such a woman should die by strangling. Ezekiel, an exile in Babylon, did condemn the harlot to be stripped naked and stoned (Ezek. 16:28-40). We do not know that this ever took place in Israel. In the New Testament (John 8:4-5) the scribes and Pharisees reminded Jesus that a woman guilty of this sin should be stoned.

Pusey points out two types of nakedness—outward and inward. The outward nakedness occurs when one is deprived of this world's goods or status; the inward, when one's soul is stripped of God's glory and grace.[2] Since the nation had despised God's grace and glory, she was to be stripped of all God's gifts. The word translated "set" (v. 3) means "fix." This verb speaks of Israel's lack of strength to free herself from judgment. She was to remain helpless as others gazed upon her.

When the Israelites were brought out of Egypt, they had no houses.

In fact, they possessed few earthly goods. Hosea wrote that this low and hard way of life would return. The glory of the land would be gone; the soil no longer would be fertile. Fruitful fields would become dreary deserts. Israel would not meet her death by strangling or stoning; she would die of thirst. There was a drought of desire for the word of the Lord in Hosea's day. Another kind of drought would arise: Israel would thirst for the physical necessities of life.

The statement that God would have no mercy upon the harlot's children does not refer to Gomer's offspring. Hosea was speaking rather of the people who lived in the land. A generation that did not know God had arisen. These people were not stable because they had no deep roots. It sobers us when we think that we ourselves are always only one generation from being pagan. If we fail to win people to Christ in our day and Christ delays his return, there will be no Christians to follow us when we die. This failure to win the next generation happened to Israel. For that reason the nation's doom was sealed.

Hosea was silent here about the details of Israel's shameful conduct. His silence makes Israel's disgrace the more intense. Israel had renounced her true God and defiled the land openly. To understand this fact, we must come back again to the nature of Baal worship in Israel during Hosea's day. The people carried their heads proudly and boasted loudly. They were not conscious of great sin. Jehovah was still their normal God. They thought, however, that he was not able to give them all the things they needed. They looked at their situation with hardheaded common sense, they thought. Where Baal made no claim, God was worshiped. And each was worshiped according to the appropriate rituals. The people saw nothing wrong in bringing new ideas such as sex acts into their worship.

Israel's lovers were not the nearby nations such as Egypt and Assyria. At certain times during Israel's past she had courted the favor of these nations. Here, though, Hosea referred to Israel's union with the temple priestesses of Baal. By so doing, Israel thought to assure the fertility of field and flock.

The worship of the people cried out against Israel. It stamped her as a vile harlot. Israel disgusted God by her forward and pushy way of life. The word "go" (v. 5) pictures Israel as not waiting to be enticed, allured, or seduced. Rather, she made the first approach. The Hebrew word translated "lovers" (v. 5) contains the idea of intense passion. The plural form implies more than one lover.

When love for God vanishes, human weakness with all its frailties enters. Israel gave her lovers credit for bringing six things. They are set forth in three couplets. The bread and water (v. 5) refer to the food that sustains life. This is followed by wool and flax (v. 5), which clothe the body. The oil and drink (v. 5) may be thought of as luxuries. Oil may mean perfumes, although it may refer also to items of healing for the body. In this context the Hebrew word for "drink" is plural, and refers to wine or fermented liquors made from such fruits as the date, mulberry, fig, and dried raisin. One is amazed to observe how many times the Bible speaks of wine and strong drink as that which degrades.

Israel's guilt was caused by more than her desire for things. She was guilty because she credited her blessings to Baal, not to Jehovah God. The one supreme God called for righteous living, but Baal did not. Followers of Baal believed sexual relations with shrine priestesses proper and right in any Baal shrine. Thus sexual immorality was rampant in the land.

When one ceases to be grateful to God for his blessings, there is no limit to the depths he may sink in vile living.

2. Results of the Bride's Faithless Conduct *(2:6-13)*

Hosea wrote that God would take steps to make Israel see the folly of her ways. Four results of Israel's sin are mentioned in verses 6-13. (See the four subheads of this section of the textbook.) Also two statements of what the Lord intended to do with Israel are made. These are prefaced by the word "therefore" (vv. 6,9). A third statement (v. 14) begins with this same word. Here we will treat verses 6-13 as one unit and approach verses 14-23 separately.

Disappointment (2:6-7)

Israel's lust drove her to discover two amazing facts. First, she was not free from Jehovah's punishment. Second, her lovers could not bless her as she had assumed. She did not conclude, as did the prodigal son,[3] that she should come back to the One who truly loved her. Israel remained stubborn. This forced the Lord to action. In verse 6 the verbs which describe God's action express God's purpose for the immediate future. His judgments will be swift and certain.

The phrase "hedge up" (v. 6) is not applied to a traveler who has lost his way, but to one who finds a thorn hedge planted across it. The wall (which involves the second verb) might have been scaled through a breach in former days. Now it was built up solidly and could not be scaled. This work was done by the true God. He must chastise his people. He will send a dark event to paralyze their vital powers.

The hedge is a picture of how God works with his people. He never remains aloof. Although he may seem to be unaware, he is not. The true Christian can never enjoy sinful ways. When he does wrong, he proceeds down a blind alley. Plans which are opposed to God's will lead in the end to an impasse. The road is blocked because the goal we have chosen is opposed to God's purpose for us.

The words "follow" and "seek" (v. 7) show intense action. Israel will search frantically for happiness. She will leave no means untried to reach her lovers. Destined to frustration, she will know futility. She will no longer feel her lovers' mystic presence. They will have vanished from her, and the blessings they were supposed to have given will no longer exist.

What was to happen? God would withdraw his hand and leave Israel to herself. No one is more hopeless than one who is alone—without God. Yet sometimes God must withdraw to bring us to our senses. The prodigal son went into the far country. His father could no longer protect him. Away from the father's presence and protection, the prodigal came to his senses. So it was with Israel.

What about Israel's motive (v. 7) as she chose to return to God? Was she sincere, or did she merely desire something better? Did she really mean it, or was it merely remorse because the other gods had failed? The matter of our true motive is a subtle one. No one likes to be loved merely because of what he does for another—not even God. Yet all our motives are mixed. Our best desires are often streaked with base alloy. One fact comforts us: Our motives are not all bad. Lessons we learned the hard way still teach us. Even fear can be a proper motive. God deals with us where we are and on the level where we live. Israel's motives were mingled, but so are ours. We must remain grateful that God accepts all of us, even with our less than pure motives. This fact is a part of his amazing grace and reconciling love.

Spiritual Blindness (2:8)

How could Israel have failed to be aware of the source of her blessings? The clause "she did not know" (v. 8) is echoed in the climax of this section (v. 13). There the prophet said that Israel "ran after her lovers and forgot me" (NEB). Israel was blind because she refused to admit that God supplied her needs. At the root of such action is always a stubborn self-will.

Israel had no excuse for her failure to give glory to God. It was he, not Baal, who gave the land and its produce. The book of

Deuteronomy records an ancient custom of worship. A man brought his firstfruits to God. He then confessed both his need for God and how grateful he was to him (Deut. 26:1-11). Through Israel's history she had been taught it was the Lord who met all her needs. In Hosea's day Israel did more than divide her loyalties. She denied the whole basis on which the nation's history had been built. In her denial she was failing to accept Jehovah himself as her Lord. It was more than not knowing the source of her blessings. Israel had put Jehovah out of her life. She did not "know" because she had been deceived by the glamour and shallow nature of false worship. Why does man fail in any period of time? It is because he is not able or willing to admit he is a creature, not the Creator. Man depends upon God for all things. When man fails to admit this, he finds that walls which cannot be scaled will block his true progress.

Benefits Removed (*2:9-12*)

When Hosea spoke the words of verses 9-12, the people were far from coming back to God. Drastic action had to be taken. To teach Israel the truth, Jehovah had to take away the good things from her life. In verse 9 we have the word "my" used four times. This shows a strong protest by the prophet against the basic concept of Baal worship. These blessings were Jehovah's; he could withdraw them at any moment. The phrase "uncover her lewdness in the sight of her lovers" (v. 10) does not mean Hosea believed lesser gods really lived. He used a device of style to attract a hearing. Hosea's point was that those gods whom Israel thought to be strong were without power to render any help. Her disgrace would come when she was exposed in public. This exposure would take place in the sight of other nations, before Canaanite worshipers. The good things she enjoyed would be depleted, and her status clearly set forth. Perhaps then she would become aware of the true source of her blessings.

Hosea had nothing but disgust for the religious feast days of Israel. They had become nothing but sex orgies. The two forms of worship standing side by side in Israel meant many Canaanite customs had come into Israel's sacred days. After the northern and southern tribes had parted, both kept the feast days. There were three great feasts: Unleavened Bread, Firstfruits, and Ingathering (Ex. 23:14-17). The term "new moons" (v. 11) refers to the early custom of observing the first day of the month as sacred. Even some of Israel's neighbors adopted this practice. The "sabbaths" (v. 11) were also holy. Proper conduct on the sabbath was commanded. The phrase "solemn assemblies" (v. 11) is a term for all the feasts not mentioned by the prophet.

What was Hosea saying? Hosea's point was that the levity and wild conduct connected with religious holidays would be removed. Israel would see how great had been her crime against God. When judgment fell, the people would awake to their senses. There would be a new basis as well as a new method for coming to God in worship. What would Hosea say today if he could see the modern-day drinking parties at our Christmas season? Would he not cry out against us also?

In Palestine the vine and fig tree (v. 12) were two plants which brought great delight. To destroy them would have been a serious blow. Joel spoke with alarm of the time when they would be taken away from Israel (1:7). They were plentiful, and they stood for luxury. Thus the people looked at them in a special way. The plants seemed to confirm the rightness of Israel's Baal worship.

Hosea saw the vine and fig tree as symbols of wicked living. When a Baal worshiper paid the shrine priestess a fee for her services, the worshiper felt his entire action assured fertility. But the whole concept was opposed to the very basic idea of a holy God. When Jehovah gave his blessing, he wanted the people to be grateful, live cleanly, and insist on justice in the land. Because Israel had sold out to the Canaanite myth, she must meet Jehovah in judgment. The gardens would grow up in thickets. They would become dwelling places of wild animals. Israel would see how foolish she had been to forget her true husband, the Creator and Redeemer. She would know that he alone is the giver of good things.

Divine Punishment (2:13)

To Hosea, the word "forgat" (v. 13) meant to betray all things for which Jehovah stood. It meant both "to ignore" and "to rebel against" his saving acts in Israel's history. Such conduct must be dealt with in a drastic and public manner. The word "visit" (v. 13) means "punish," and most versions render it this way.

The "earrings" (v. 13) (alternate reading: "nose rings") and jewels were not to attract the lovers. Rather, the reference is to the custom of dressing oneself in his best garments for the holy days. More than dressing up in one's best was in this custom. Clothes worn in day-to-day duties were washed before they were worn to worship. Otherwise, they would defile the place of worship. Also clothes made holy by contact with holy things were taboo in daily life. Thus Israel had gone all out in her Baal worship. She should have seen that the merger of Jehovah worship with the Baal was absurd. She had been blind and stupid. Now no way to escape the divine harvest was open. The God who is ignored in daily living is unavoidable in judgment.

3. The Heart of the Forgiving Companion (*2:14-20*)

Israel's plight in judgment moved God to loving concern. This passage shows God's grace in dealing with Israel and her glory beyond judgment. God's promise to Israel is his promise to us too.

A Renewed Wooing (*2:14-15*)

To the prophets, Israel's best days were when she was led by Moses through Sinai. This time was the honeymoon between Israel and her God. Things had changed since. Matters had become so urgent that God must step in with direct action.

Notice that verse 14 begins with "therefore," and thus suggests a relationship between verses 2-13 and 14-15. The word may refer in a special way to the last phrase in verse 13. The people may have forgotten the Lord, but he will not forget them. The verb should be rendered, "I am about to allure her." This rendering means that God would act very soon.

The word "wilderness" (v. 14) refers, most likely, to the Exile. When the foreign power was through with his work, the land would be so torn up that people could not live in it. The phrase "speak comfortably" (v. 14) means "speak to the heart." The prophet was saying God would be so tender when he entreated Israel that she would come to depend upon him to the fullest. God's words would comfort Israel; he would assure her of his loving presence.

Verse 15 should be looked at against the background of Achan's great sin (Josh. 7:1-26). The Valley of Achor is on the northern boundary of Judah. It runs from ancient Jericho into the hills and forms a passage from the Jordan valley to the upper region. This valley is the normal entrance into Canaan. A tragic thing occurred here in the early days. Achan was guilty of a great sin, and Israel lost the battle with Ai because of it. When Joshua brought the sin to light, Achan and his family were put to death in this valley. Achan's sin with its just deserts was a terrible thing to happen just as the Israelites were going into the Promised Land! God's harsh judgment upon sin grieved them greatly, but taught them a needed lesson.

This time, so that they would learn a great truth, God would cause the people to suffer. God's purpose was to redeem the world through them. They must be humbled in order that they might become the kind of people he could use. The Exile would be God's means of bringing the defiled bride to purity. Beyond judgment Israel would have a future without limit.

Hosea's vision of the future reflected his assurance. This passage in the Old Testament is close to the gospel of Jesus Christ. The expression "she shall make answer" (v. 15) is rendered "shall sing" in older versions. This may be the best meaning for the context. The picture is that of people singing back and forth to each other. The new exodus will be a joyful affair. God's erring people will be happy. The anguish of exile will be turned by God into the joy of forgiveness.

Hardship does not always turn people back to the Lord. Sometimes it makes them bitter. More often, though, our tears become telescopes through which we more clearly see our God. Truths obscured in the noontime of affluence become clear in the black midnight of suffering. God, who is light, is often found in the darkness.

A Restored Relationship (*2:16-17*)

After Israel was restored, Hosea promised, she would no longer be confused concerning the name or nature of her God. Hosea understood man must relate to God in love. He knew that if one served God in truth, he must have God's outlook in all things. This outlook included sharing with God life's goals and his ways of working to reach them.

Closely tied as it was to Canaanite worship, the word "Baal" came to convey unwholesome religion. The phrase "at that day" (v. 16) was used often by the prophets, and stood for the time when God would act decisively. It would be action either to judge or to save. Hosea saw that in the future God would remove the love of idols from Israel's heart. She would no longer call Baal her husband (Ishi, KJV).

A New Hope for Peace (*2:18*)

Although this passage seems to refer to Israel only, it extends beyond her. The Lord will create a new environment in which lasting peace can prevail. Even the beasts, birds, and creeping things will join their efforts in the venture.

Here, as often in the Old Testament prophets, we see a blending of time and eternity into one vivid portrait. Hosea always saw the ideal coming to pass. He connected the peace between man and beasts with the time when peace would prevail among men. No weapons would be needed then.

It is not required that we make all these passages refer to a golden age after our Lord's second coming. Men of goodwill find joy in working for peace among men in their own day. For us to strive for an ideal even though we know we shall never quite attain it is good. We know perfect peace will not prevail until God himself steps in and brings it to us in a dramatic fashion by Christ's own presence. This does not mean, however, that we should put forth no efforts of our own to bring peace among men.

Hosea contended that when men come to know the Lord in love, society will be better. Indeed this is the only hope we have for bringing hostile people closer to each other in daily living. God's kingdom is love. Neither mighty armies nor mind-boggling defense systems will make us secure. When people love the same God and share the same ideals, they can live without war. This ideal is our true and only hope for a lasting peace. That fact makes evangelizing all the nations a must.

A New Wedding (2:19-20)

For an Israelite, betrothal meant more than engagement means to us today. Betrothal was the final step before the marriage was consummated. It involved the payment for the bride. Both parties had agreed the wedding would take place. The marriage contract had been arranged. All that remained was a formal service and the couple's union. Hosea used the word "betroth" three times in verses 19-20. God had made up his mind to perform his purpose with regard to Israel.

This new marriage would be based on two great virtues. The word "righteousness" (v. 19) relates very closely to Jehovah's saving work. Righteousness can become real when one is personally related to God, who energizes for living and motivates conduct. The word "justice" (v. 19) has to do with one's rights and duties. Only a lasting knowledge of and love for God can reconcile rights and duties so that justice is produced. God is the true source of just relations among men.

"Lovingkindness" and "mercies" (v. 19) complete the picture of the new marriage between God and his people. These virtues make sure the union will be a lasting one. The passing of years will not affect it. The ravages of time will not sever the bride and groom. This new bond will endure in cordial and caring love. The new spirit will make itself felt in every area of life. It will create something new, something never known in the past.

The climax of the relationship will come in the effects produced by it. The chief result will be the "faithfulness" (v. 20) that will come. The Hebrew word "faithful" means "steadfast," and is related to moral trustworthiness and integrity in all matters. One who is rightly related to God will show forth in his life those things which are pleasing to God. The Lord will expect Israel to be morally pure and emotionally steadfast. The discipline of the Exile will do for Israel what the memory of the Exodus had not. Israel will become faithful.

The verb "know" is used often in the Old Testament to describe the sex act in marriage. This does not mean, though, that we should read this meaning into verse 20. The prophet opposed this part of Baal worship with all his strength. The word should be understood to express the depth of the feeling between God and his people in their new bond. When we know someone, we are aware of his full nature. The word conveys the concept of sharing the goals of one's life with another in a living way. The moral change which would come to Israel would cause her to adopt God's view, especially in the moral and spiritual issues of life.

To know and to love are very closely related. We cannot really love someone until we know him. On the other hand, neither can we know him unless we love him. The more we know someone, the greater our ability to love him. Also the more we love someone, the deeper our knowledge of him. God has joined these two virtues. Man cannot and should not try to separate them. He can and should experience them in his relation to God.

4. Reversal of Previous Decrees *(2:21-23)*

The prophet saw beyond judgment to future blessings for Israel. Verses 9,12 present a dreary picture, but they are not the full story. The prophet looked forward to a time when all the spheres of life would work in order. Then the Lord's restraint on nature's powers would be unnecessary. Neither would Israel be shamed in the sight of her neighbors through God's refusal to claim and present her as his own. The threats would be voided. God would call upon the forces of nature to work as one. He would resolve to vindicate his people in the sight of the nations. He would call upon people and land alike to come to his aid.

Land Will Be Blessed (2:21-22)

What was the goal of Baal worship? It was to assure that the land would be fertile. Jehovah alone could make fertility a reality. He would in the future lead each part of nature's cycle to respond to the other. But Hosea's God of love would reach beyond the human realm. Both man and nature would have a part in God's purpose. Each part would respond to the other. Each would work in the divine venture to make God's creation function as God had intended.

New Meanings for Names (2:23)

Although the word "Jezreel" (v. 22) means "scatter," it can also mean "sow." The prophet used both meanings in this verse. In some ways the meanings are similar, yet in other ways they are dissimilar. God would no longer scatter his people. They would be ready now to take root and grow. He had reconciled them. The fact that they had been renewed would make possible a wondrous harvest. Whereas God had almost given up his people and refused to show mercy, he in the future would know fulfillment. He would win them to himself through his endless love. His grace would break down everything that stood between him and his people. They would return to him. Mercy and pardon would be given. Every barrier would be removed. The best of all, they would be his people once more, and this time they would never leave.

The gospel truth of God's reconciling love is found as clearly in Hosea as in any other part of the Old Testament. The redeemed family of God is his true people. It is not by works of righteousness that they have done. (See Titus 3:5.) It is God's gracious love that does not let go until it has triumphed. The sinner is brought home to peace, joy, and service. God's redemptive purpose will be accomplished. How thrilling it is for us to be a part of it!

5. Lessons for Life from the Scriptures

This heartrending poem on the husbandhood of God contains some soul-searching lessons of great value for modern living.

Unclean living is an awful thing! This is a day when we have become concerned about pollution in the physical world. It is indeed a problem. Every Christian has a duty to help keep the world clean. An even worse problem is unclean living. God's Word teaches us a Christian should stay apart from the sinful things of this world. One of the most tragic sights to be found today is a person who has defiled his body. When this happens, all other types of decay come quickly.

We cannot serve two gods at the same time. The mind cannot function properly when two opposing values seek to control it. We cannot be like Bunyan's Mr. Facing-Both-Ways of *The Pilgrim's*

Progress. Jesus must be lord of all, or he will not be lord at all. A man seeking to serve two masters may be like the Dead Sea, which reflects heaven on its surface, but hides Gomorrah in its heart.

The things of the world do not bring real joy. One who seeks his good times in the things of this life never has enough of them. It always takes more next time to bring a thrill. Only in Jesus do we find the peace that brings perfect joy and makes us truly happy. The world can neither give this kind of peace nor take it away.

A wise person will never forget the source of his blessings. For one to forget who gives him his good things is a base sin. William Pitt, Prime Minister of England, became bitter when his friends forgot the favors he did for them. He wrote about it with strong feeling. If divine gifts are forgotten in human ingratitude, the next step is to forget the Giver. All things come to us from the hand of a kind and gracious God.

God is always seeking the sinner. No one goes so far in sin that he is beyond God's grace. Long before we turn to God, he seeks us. He has placed churches in many places in order that lost people might be reached. He has laid upon the hearts of concerned people to share the gospel message. God will not quit in his endless quest for the one who has left him and gone astray. Some religions are based on man's seeking a god, but Christianity is founded upon God's seeking man.

To chastise sinning man is part of God's plan for making him better. The valley of suffering always points to a door of hope. We must know the shadows before we truly can love the sunshine. God is on the field even when we cannot see him. He is working out his purposes in the lives of both nations and individuals. The dark threads are needed to make life's pattern beautiful.

---

[1] The title of this chapter is a variation of the title of a hymn by George Matheson, "O Love That Wilt Not Let Me Go," in *Baptist Hymnal*, ed. William J. Reynolds (Nashville: Convention Press, 1975), p. 368.

[2] Pusey, *op. cit.*, p. 29.

[3] Luke 15:11-32.

PERSONAL LEARNING ACTIVITIES

1. Four results of Israel's sin as set out in verses 6-13 are (check the correct responses):

____ (1) Disappointment ____ (4) Irreligion

____ (2) Sickness
____ (3) Spiritual blindness
____ (5) Benefits removed
____ (6) Divine punishment

2. In Hosea 2:15 the prophet referred to (check correct response):
    ____ (1) Achan's sin
    ____ (2) Valley of Achor
    ____ (3) The conquest of Canaan

Answers:

1. (1), (3), (5), (6); 2. (2).

4
"Did E'er Such Love and Sorrow Meet?" [1]

HOSEA 3:1-5; 1:10 to 2:1

The account in 3:1-5 should be studied after that in 1:2-9. We cannot be certain how much time elapsed between the two events. The wife who had left her husband had now sunk to the lowest levels of shame and disgrace. In this section Hosea told the story himself. There is no need to discuss the style of writing nor the change from third to first person pronouns. The chapter gives intimate detail and contains facts only Hosea would have known. The account must have come from his own hand since it came so directly from his heart.

Chapter 3 is in many ways the heart of the book. All Hosea said in his future messages is molded in this event. The sinful woman stands for Israel. Hosea's ransom speaks of God's love for his people. In no Old Testament passage do we feel any nearer to Calvary than here. In Hosea's purchase of Gomer for silver and grain, we see Christ's ransom of the sinner from sin.

The redeemed harlot had to be disciplined, a fact which speaks in symbol of Israel's future. She too must go through a period of cleansing. Only then would she be able to serve her Lord again. Repentance never is easy; it comes into a life only in response to an overwhelming love. That is the story of Gomer's repentance, of Israel's, and of every sinner's.

In the text, of course, 1:10 to 2:1 follows the account of the three children's births. There is no reason to assume, as some have done, that this passage is a misplaced fragment. It goes well exactly where it is. Most likely, Gomer left home shortly after the birth of her third child. These three verses are thus a comfort to the bereaved husband at that time in his life. The reason we deferred consideration of this passage until now is in order that we might have a logical approach to Hosea's preaching and Israel's history. We can in this way combine the two related thoughts of reconciliation and restoration.

1. A Second Difficult Command to the Prophet (*3:1*)

Once more God commanded Hosea to make his own life a means of bringing divine truth to the nation. He was told to seek reconciliation with Gomer, who at that time was guilty of unclean conduct. He was to show the people the depth of God's love for them. This drama, acted out in Hosea's life, is the basis of his book. Every salient theme of the prophet's oracles is contained in this command and his doing it.

Most interpreters agree the word "again" (3:1) refers to the command to "go love" rather than "said." In the Hebrew the word translated "again" (3:1) appears before the two verbs. This construct gives the word a strong force. The word could be translated by our word "still," an appropriate translation since the woman is the same as the one in chapter 1. That rendering fits the symbol. There is no record Hosea ever divorced Gomer. He remained faithful all through the period in which she loved others. Likewise God never fully cast off Israel. The symbol is ideal in showing how God refused because of his great love to abandon his bride Israel.

The phrase "a woman beloved of her friend" (v. 1) is not easy to translate. The Revised Standard Version has "beloved of a paramour." The actual Hebrew seems best brought into English as "a woman loved of her lover." We may see this woman as one who was guilty of a loose sex life. The point is clear. Hosea was told by God to seek out his wife who was living an impure life. The first chapter, which implies strongly Gomer left her home to follow more freely her shameful deeds, corresponds with this interpretation.

God's love for Israel was in spite of her sin. Hosea's phrase "other gods" (v. 1) clearly refers to Baal worship. He spoke of the people as loving "flagons of wine" (v. 1, KJV) or "cakes of raisins" (v. 1, RSV), a clear reference to the dainty food which was made of dried grapes. These sweet cakes were often used in the feasts of cultic worship. Jeremiah referred to cakes made of dough offered to Astarte, queen of heaven (7:18; 44:19). Small carved figures of the goddess Astarte, which show her holding a round object, have been found. The object was, no doubt, a raisin cake of the type mentioned by Hosea. In that day, the eating of these cakes was a part of the Baal worship service. The people believed these pagan gods gave the vintage, and the raisin cakes were offered in worship. They were thanking the gods, but later they ate the cakes themselves.

Hosea was speaking in a caustic manner. The sweetness of the wine-soaked food appealed to the carnal nature of the people. Their impulses and desires were stimulated by the sex element in Baal worship. This pagan worship service clearly was designed to appeal to the passions of man's lower nature. The worshiper was not helped; he was hurt.

God's command was difficult for the prophet. Sometimes a woman forgives an erring man. Not as many times a man forgives a faithless wife. Hosea was one of the latter few. He may have forgiven Gomer because he yearned to, but that is guesswork. We know Hosea felt that his forgiveness of Gomer was God's will.

Two simple truths emerge from God's command to Hosea. First, God demands complete loyalty. We seem to hear the first of the Ten Commandments in God's reminder to Hosea that Israel had been untrue. Second, Hosea perceived divine truth through his own experience. In the events of chapter 1 Hosea learned from Gomer's faithlessness how God suffers when men turn away from him. In the events of chapter 3, Hosea learned from God's faithfulness with Israel the necessity of his faithfulness to lost Gomer. In her reclamation Hosea learned firsthand how love hurts while it heals.

2. The Prophet's Prompt Obedience (*3:2*)

Why was Hosea required to purchase the woman? It could be Hosea did not wish to have any quarrel with Gomer's lover. Another possible answer to the question is based on the meaning of the verb "bought" (v. 2). The Hebrew word does not always mean purchase. It could mean here that Hosea arranged for Gomer's upkeep over a limited period of time. Some interpreters suggest he brought silver and food to be used for her until he could restore her to wifehood. However, this solution does not have much support. The preferred meaning of the verb is "bought," and most likely it should be rendered that way in this passage. The answer to our question may be hidden in the price Hosea paid for the woman.

How much did Hosea pay for Gomer? The fifteen pieces of silver were coins, each equal to a shekel. The value of the grain was equal to fifteen shekels also. Thus Hosea paid thirty shekels for Gomer—the price of a slave. Gomer had probably become a slave-concubine of some man. To reclaim her, Hosea first had to buy her.

We immediately think of our Master, who was betrayed for thirty pieces of silver (Matt. 27:3). What a contrast in the two! Gomer was enslaved by sin. Most likely she had gone as deeply into sin of the flesh as a woman can go. On the other hand, our Savior knew no sin. He was made to be sin on our behalf, that "we might become the righteousness of God in him" (2 Cor. 5:21).

Hosea was not obliged in any way to Gomer. The law of the land said he could have had her stoned. Hosea has been called the prophet of love. He is more. He is the prophet of unrequited love. He loved even though he was spurned.

Likewise Christ died for us even while we spurned his love. But God extends his love to us even when we do not deserve it. This is the very essence of the Christian gospel.

The story seems to suggest that for Hosea to raise the purchase price was not easy. Exodus 21:32 tells us thirty shekels was the price of a female slave. We read in Judges 17:10 that Micah's priest was paid ten shekels a year, plus his clothes and upkeep. This seems to suggest that if Hosea was merely a peasant farmer-preacher, thirty shekels would be a large sum. Perhaps this is why he finished the payment with grain. Roy Honeycutt says: "It was at considerable price for a poor man of the eighth century that Hosea redeemed his wife. He expended his accumulated possessions in exchange for one who had despised him publicly." [2] Hosea's love seems to have God's love in it. It was a love that outlived and outgave all reasonable human expectations.

3. The Limits of Liberty (3:3)

There are always restraints to our freedom. God's grace must discipline. This is as much a part of his work of redemption as his forgiveness. No battle is won without effort. The sinful woman found mercy. She was brought back to her wronged husband, but she had to pay a price. All the marriage relationships were not resumed at once. The prophet must first of all see whether or not she could accept the guidelines required in this way of life. Was she mature enough now to be faithful? Would she want to wander once more? There is no record that she passed the test. Our Christian idealism leads us to believe the best about her.

Hosea's statement in verse 3 does not mean God's forgiveness has conditions other than repentance and faith. We are dealing with a real-life situation. In ancient Israel a marriage followed the pattern of the ancient cultures. Romance between marriage partners counted little. At the outset a man chose a woman for marriage because she had the potential of fulfilling certain basic economic, social, and physical needs. This may have been true at first with Hosea.

(In 1:2 he was told to take a wife.) However, later Hosea was moved by deeper concerns. (In 3:1 he was told to "love a woman.") A marriage might begin for fleshly reasons, but it must become more. A love that transcends the needs of the flesh must arise. Hosea's long-range aim was to have Gomer share his life. In this second venture with her, Hosea was more cautious. He needed to be convinced she was ready to settle down and accept maturely the demands of marriage.

During this period Gomer was required to be quiet and stable, a departure from her recent past. The restraint was to have great teaching value. She would learn passions of the flesh are to be controlled. One cannot have every desire fulfilled on the spur of the moment. This, of course, meant the prophet was to be deprived also of the physical aspects of married life. In order to cure her of a wayward life, he must also practice personal restraint. An incidental lesson emerges here. No married person has the right to engage in loose sex because of a partner's guilt. Any type of revenge is wrong—particularly that of getting even with a faithless partner in the marriage relationship.

How do the facts of Hosea's life at this point apply to God's dealings with Israel? God is faithful to his bride. He will not experiment with Babylon or Egypt during the time he must chastise Israel. He has promised to bless the world through the seed of Abraham. He will not cast off the people when they rebel, even though he may feel like it.

This passage emphasizes a sublime truth about the true nature of love. It is not blind. No one knows a person's faults more than the other member of the marriage. Love accepts and works with the raw product in order to make it stronger and better. On the other hand, love must demand. No one respects weakness. We gain strength only from the strong. True love must stand as a bulwark. The weak member of a marriage draws strength from the resources of the partner. Thus each partner in marriage accepts the other and extends to the other a redemptive, caring love. Together each is stronger than either is alone.

4. Application to Israel (*3:4-5*)

Verse 3 ends the story of Hosea's tragic marriage and homelife. In the next two verses he relates his experience to the life of the nation. Israel's supreme need was for a new spirit. She, like Gomer, had to be secluded until her sense of values had been restored. She would be deprived in this period of all functions necessary to the civil life and worship. Jehovah would bring the people to their senses. A time in the future would come when they would enjoy fellowship once again with their God.

Hosea mentions six things through which Israel must "sit still" (the true meaning of "abide" [v. 4]) during the exile. They may be placed in three sets of two each. The first pair ("King . . . prince," [v. 4]) relates to the ruling of the land. The "sacrifice, and . . . pillar" (v. 4) stand for public worship, which had become perverted through the Baal influences. The "ephod or teraphim" (v. 4) refers to private worship, which also had suffered abuse at the hand of those who worshiped idols.

Hosea spoke mainly to the Northern Kingdom. We can see easily he had little or no use for their rulers. He put all of them in the same class as Jeroboam I, who usurped ten tribes. His scorn does not mean Hosea was against rulers. He knew a nation must have leaders. In the future Israel's kings would be removed as punishment, not blessing, to the nation. Any nation without a leader is in peril. True, Israel's kings deserved to be dethroned. But when God did this, he indicted the nation, not the government. There is nothing in the words of Hosea to support doing away with central authority in public life.

The pillars were symbols of the divine presence. They were stones erected at any place where the one who worshiped felt God had clearly shown his presence and power. The Hebrews had erected pillars at such places as Shechem (Josh. 24:26), Mizpah (1 Sam. 7:12), Gibeon (2 Sam. 20:8), Bethel (Gen. 28:18), Gilead (Gen. 31:45), Gilgal (Josh. 4:5), and En-rogel (1 Kings 1:9). The tragedy was that these pillars had been taken over by cultic worship and had become places for sexual orgies. The prophets spoke severely against these things. The merging of Jehovah worship and the Baal had brought the pillars into low esteem. The prophet felt that in order to keep the worship pure they must be removed from the land.

Both the ephod and the teraphim were used in private worship to discover the divine will. We cannot be certain as to the full meaning of the ephod. The word seems to be used in the Old Testament two different ways. In many passages it was a piece of clothing worn by the priests, and sometimes by others, in worship. It was a sleeveless coat. On it were lovely and costly materials. It contained a pouch for stones which were used in an effort to divine the future.

In other passages the ephod seems to have been an image which was worshiped. The root meaning of the word is "to cover." Some have suggested that in these uses the ephod was an image of Jehovah covered with silver and gold.

Both meanings most likely are valid uses of the word. In some cases the ephod functioned as a garment, while in others it was an image, either large or small. They were of different sizes and weights. Thus the ephod could be carried, or placed as a large object on the wall. On the other hand, the use did not vary. It was designed to find what course of action one should take. The ephod claimed to direct the one who worshiped, and help him find the divine will for his future actions.

The teraphim were household gods. They were first used in ancestor worship. Like the ephod, they were consulted for knowledge of the future and the course of action one should pursue. The word occurs only in the plural form. They were similar to pennants and often contained images of ancestors.

One should not conclude Hosea approved the use of these things. He did connect them with king, prince, and sacrifice. He saw them as items which had been a part of the nation's culture. He was, no doubt, speaking with scorn when he declared they would be taken away from the people. To Hosea, the ephod and teraphim were crude forms for use in seeking God's will. He also saw the corrupt things which were present at the sacrifices. The great worth of the exile to Israel would be that she would look again at her values and decide which things to keep. Worship would become an experience of the spirit, and the false worship which corrupted the nation and its institutions would be excised.

The fifth verse begins and ends with a note of hope for the future. Although the immediate future looked dark, Hosea saw hope beyond. His greatest virtue was faith. He was certain God's love would triumph. The expression "the latter days" (v. 5) speaks of a time when God will act in history to fulfill his purpose. It will be the golden age of the messiah, the time when God's revealed will will be full and complete. Men can live in the hope of its coming.

The two words "return" and "seek" (v. 5) are used in the same manner, although their root meanings vary slightly. The Hebrew word rendered "return" has within it the same idea as the New Testament word "repent." It is a word rich in meaning and always suggests some type of renewal. The word rendered "seek" is a technical term. It is used for one's seeking to find God through worship ritual. Its meaning varies in Old Testament usage, but here it has high ethical content. In this context the word has nothing to do with coming to God through the cultic forms of Baal worship, but suggests an intense and zealous spiritual quest.

Two main Hebrew words for "fear" are found in the Old Testament. One of them is more often used and suggests "reverence," "awe," and "honor." The word used in verse 5 is much stronger. It speaks of dread or terror. A two-fold picture of Israel's return is suggested. First, the people come trembling. They are keenly aware that God is holy, and they are not worthy because of their sins. As they think how helpless they are, anguish and distress fill them. (This agrees with two other statements of Hosea [5:15; 11:11].) This fear, though, blocks their approach to God. Something more is needed—"goodness" (v. 5). Fear had its part in moving them to action, but it was God's goodness which encouraged them to approach him. Paul spoke of God's goodness as leading man to repent (Rom. 2:4). Fear may drive a person to realize his need for the Lord. It is God's goodness which will lead him to give himself fully to God's will.

What did Hosea mean by "David their king" (v. 5)? Of course, he was not saying the ancient monarch would be raised from the dead and rule once again over Israel. Nor should we think of this as a charge against the Northern Kingdom for having refused the rule of Rehoboam, the son of Solomon, when the kingdom split in 931 B.C. Hosea's feeling for the rulers of the Northern Kingdom was based on their lack of moral fiber. More interpreters agree that the David Hosea mentioned is the messiah. The ideal king of the future would be a second David.

We cannot be sure what the people thought when they heard Hosea speak those words. Many good Jews of that day thought of the messiah as a political ruler. In fact, this was the basic belief about the messiah in the days when Jesus was on earth. However, Christians know—in the light of the New Testament—that Hosea's words were fulfilled truly in the coming of Jesus Christ. (See Matt. 1:1-17; 21:9; Luke 1:30-33; 3:23-38.) Any other idea falls short of the deeper and true meaning of Hosea's words.

5. Future Restoration for Israel (*1:10 to 2:1*)

For a nation to have many citizens was important in Hosea's day. As Hosea viewed the future, he saw a new nation with a large population. Those things God had promised to Abraham and Jacob (Gen. 22:17; 32:12) had been only partly realized. The nation would indeed go into exile, but a nucleus would return. From this small group a mighty people would emerge. Hosea saw a day when Israel's population would be so great that the people could not be numbered.

The resources of God's grace would bring to Israel light out of darkness, joy out of sorrow, and life out of death. In contrast to the present plight, a time was coming when Israel would be fertile and produce countless children. God would not allow his chosen nation to perish from the earth. He had a purpose for them, and it would be fulfilled.

If one looked casually at the situation in Hosea's day, he might have believed God had forsaken his people. They were no longer worthy to be called sons of God (v. 10). Hosea, however, believed things would change! Israel would once more be seen as a people who related in a unique way to their God. Where would this occur? Bible students do not agree fully on the meaning of the phrase "in the place where it was said" (v. 10). The place may be either Palestine or the land where Israel was captive. One thing is certain. It is the *fact* and not the *place* which the prophet stressed as he spoke.

The discord and warfare between Israel and Judah would vanish when the future's veil had been pushed aside and God's will had come to pass. The breach that had brought such havoc to the people would be healed. This would do away with much that had hindered God's purpose for Israel. The fact of two nations had fragmented the progress of God's kingdom. God had, however, been faithful to his people. Now Hosea offered new hope. He looked forward to a united people under a new leader whom they would choose, and whom God would approve.

Under the guidance of this "one head" (v. 11) the people would once more enjoy an exodus from bondage. The word "Jezreel" (v. 11) would take on new meaning. It would no longer refer to disaster, but rather to victory and permanence in the Promised Land. All things would be transformed. Other words would also have new content poured into them. The dilemma of God, caused by the people's sin, would change to delight and joy. The people would know what it meant to be unified under their earthly ruler and their heavenly Father. They would greet each other with joy by the new name God had given to them. Ill omens would give way to pleasant thoughts. Pardon would be the restored nation's new theme. It would become the life-style of the redeemed nation.

Has Hosea's prophecy been fulfilled? Have these things occurred? Does there remain a time yet in the future when some of them will come to pass? This is a much argued question even among our best scholars and finest Christians.

What are the facts? Israel was captured by the Assyrians in 722 B.C. She passed off the scene as a political unit. A few of her lower class people remained in the land. Assyria sent some of her culls to the land of Israel. These mingled with the people of the land and produced a half-breed race known as the Samaritans.

Judah's doom was in three stages. One group was taken captive in 605 B.C., a second group in 597 B.C., and the final fall of the city was in 586 B.C.

In 535 B.C. the Jews in Babylon were allowed to return to their native land. Some came back, but many remained in Babylon. The group that returned built the Temple again and settled the land. They refused to allow the Samaritans to have a part in their building program or in the Temple worship. This half-breed race was never received into the fold of Judaism. By the days of Jesus the two groups were intense rivals.

What about the ten tribes who were taken to Assyria? In 612 B.C. Nineveh, the capital of the Assyrian Empire, fell to Babylon. The nation did not collapse immediately when Nineveh fell. The Assyrian armies kept on fighting. The final blow came in 605 B.C. The Babylonians dealt the Assyrians a crushing defeat at the Battle of Carchemish. The Assyrian Empire was torn apart. What happened to the Jewish captives? The truth is, we do not know. No doubt, many of them died. Many of them, we are sure, were taken to Babylon where they joined their kinsmen in exile. We do know that in the return from Babylon all twelve tribes were present. In the New Testament, Paul, speaking to Agrippa, spoke of "our twelve tribes, earnestly serving God day and night" (Acts 26:7). The revived Jewish state, after the Babylonian Exile, was looked upon as one unit with twelve tribes.

In what sense, then, were Hosea's words fulfilled by the return from Babylon? To be sure, Judah and Israel became one unit again. For the most part, it is true, they remained under foreign rule. There was only a brief time during the Maccabean period (167-63 B.C.) when they were free. First the Persians (535-331 B.C.), next the Greeks (331-167 B.C.), and finally the Romans (63 B.C.-A.D. 70) served as their rulers. In A.D. 70 the Romans crushed them, and they were scattered throughout the world, where they have remained. In recent years some have returned to their homeland, and the state of Israel has emerged again.

What about the number of people? There are many Jews in the world today. They are present in almost all countries. Do they fulfill Hosea's words? Hosea's promise of many people is followed quickly by the promise they shall be prosperous and fertile.

One must admit Israel has never realized Hosea's prophecies in a literal sense. Some scholars believe Israel's golden age is in the future. They contend Israel will turn to Christ in great numbers and enjoy a glorious period during an earthly reign of Christ.

Other equally devout and capable interpreters do not agree. They contend Hosea's promise to Israel has been fulfilled in New Testament Christianity. To them, the true Israelites are not the physical children of Abraham, but the spiritual ones. The true Israelites are they who have received Christ as Savior and have become members of God's worldwide kingdom. Paul said to the Galatians, "And if ye be Christ's, then are ye Abraham's seed, and heirs according to the promise" (Gal. 3:29, KJV). In his letter to the Romans, Paul said, "For he is not a Jew, which is one outwardly; neither is that circumcision, which is outward in the flesh: But he is a Jew which is one inwardly; and circumcision is that of the heart, in the spirit, and not in the letter; whose praise is not of men, but of God" (Rom. 2:28-29, KJV). If this school of thought be received as valid, Hosea's words have been fulfilled. Those who are born again through faith in Christ have received the promises as the true Israelites.

Which is correct? One thing is certain. Christendom will never be united on this question. Many good Christians hold to each interpretation. The Scriptures teach Christians are the true children of Abraham. There is no doubt about this fact. On the other hand, other Scripture passages seem to teach that the Jews will be saved in large numbers shortly before the return of Christ. The question of the Jew and his destiny should be left with God. It should not divide the ranks of Christendom. Our task is to preach the saving gospel of God's grace to lost people no matter who they are or where they are. Hosea's love for his wife speaks of God's eternal love in Christ for the lost. It is both our duty and our privilege as Christians today to be a part of God's plan to redeem the world. We should not let incidentals or controversial issues turn us aside from our outreach in a person-to-person ministry.

6. Lessons for Life from the Scriptures

God loves us even when we are guilty. To know that fact is a source of strength. He will never forsake us. There is an even more precious thought. God cares for us even when we have sinned against him and are in the wrong. God does not love merely the lovely. His heart goes out to those who have stumbled and fallen.

Although God loves us, we all must be disciplined. We are saved by grace. We often are purified through discipline. We must spend some time alone with God before we can go into the public place and speak for God. In this secret place, we confer with him who is not "flesh and blood" (Gal. 1:16). In so doing, we gain new insights into ourselves and new understanding about the world we live in.

God always has our best interest at heart. No one loves us as much as our heavenly Father. After all, he is our Creator and Redeemer. In his time he will visit us with blessings as he seeks to work out his purposes through us.

God's will, although sometimes difficult, is best. As long as we rebel against the goals God has for us, our lives will be miserable. In God's will are both our peace and our progress. Hosea found God's will difficult. But in the doing of God's will, he found a profound understanding of God's love for Israel and a new dimension in his own love for Gomer.

The greatest source of unity is in being properly related to God. One of our greatest problems today is that of living with each other. There is no real basis for "peace among men" (Luke 2:14, RSV) until we recognize we all belong to God. This basis is the true source of any effort to bring all of us together. We are bound in the bundle of life. We must agree on those things that matter most. Above everything else, we must see our responsibility to carry the gospel, which "has broken down the dividing wall of hostility" (Eph. 2:14, RSV), to all men everywhere.

---

[1] Isaac Watts, "When I Survey the Wondrous Cross," *Baptist Hymnal, op. cit.*, p. 111.

[2] Roy L. Honeycutt, Jr., *The Broadman Bible Commentary*, Vol. 7 (Nashville: Broadman Press, 1972), pp. 18-19.

PERSONAL LEARNING ACTIVITIES

1. Hosea paid the price of a slave for Gomer's redemption. In that action and the experiences that led up to it, Hosea learned (check correct responses):
   ____ (1) God loved Israel in spite of her sin.
   ____ (2) God would utterly destroy Israel for her sin.
   ____ (3) God offered Israel redemption, and would, in spite of her sin, seek to reclaim her.
2. According to Hosea 3:4-5, what losses would Israel have to endure?

Answers:

1. (*1*), (3); 2. (1) rulers, (2) perverted public religious institutions.

5
"Where Wealth Accumulates, and Men Decay"[1]

HOSEA 4:1 to 6:3

Chapters 4—14 contain the public preaching of Hosea. No doubt, he said more, but in this section we have the essence of his entire life's work. Chapters 1—3 lay the base; they give us an intimate picture of Hosea's homelife. That which happened to him was tragic, but useful. As he looked back later, he found grist for his sermons to Israel. An outline approach to this larger section (chaps. 4—14) is found in the first chapter of this book. It will be used as a basis for a study of Hosea's recorded preaching.

Each student of Hosea presents his own outline for these messages. Few believe the chapters contain any logical order as they stand arranged in the text. This writer contends, however, that there is order, and that 4:1 to 6:3 is a distinct unit. Most likely, this passage was Hosea's first sermon to Israel. The prophet brought it during the chaotic period just after the death of Jeroboam II, when in less than a year three kings (two of whom were killed in cold blood) had come to the throne.

This sermon is, in some respects, like the first message of Jeremiah (2:1 to 4:4). It is a state-of-the-nation address. In the first five verses Hosea used a catchy device to proclaim God's message: a court of law. The legal drama is, in a way, carried through the entire chapter, although it is clearest in the first few verses. The roles shift and often overlap. This mingling does not present a problem, however. The courtroom scene is merely an analogy to the actual scene in Israel.

The people had one basic weakness from which all these symptoms sprang. They lacked a proper understanding of Jehovah's true nature. This lack had caused them to forget his unique character. Behavior that did not agree with God's holy nature had become common practice. In 4:6-14 Hosea pictured the shame that had come to the land because of the uncontrolled passions of an immoral people. A smaller section (4:15-19) concerns Judah. Hosea was, first of all, a prophet of Israel, but he was aware of and concerned with Judah's spiritual needs. As the fifth chapter begins, the prophet took a fresh start. He traced the guilt of Israel to her leaders. The people had gone so deep into sin that it seemed they were not capable of turning back. At the root of the problem was pride. The result was Israel's inability to find a meaningful fellowship with Jehovah. Judgment must come to the wicked nation, and that judgment is pictured in 5:8-15. The prophet proclaimed the coming devastation and then once more gave reasons for it. He concluded this section with a picture of the stages in God's punitive approach to the nation.

The final section in this sermon is an urgent call for Israel to look once more at herself and return to God. This heart-throbbing invitation is very much like that of Jeremiah's (4:1-4) at the close of his first sermon. Preaching should contain an appeal to repent. Mercy is available to people when they desire to return to God. This mercy is the glory of Israel's God, and of ours.

1. The Lord's Dispute with the People *(4:1-5)*

The type of preaching found in this section was a familiar format with the prophets. Isaiah (1:18-20) and Micah (6:1-5) also used the courtroom scene. The word "truth" (v. 1) was used by all three of the prophets to mean "fidelity," "consistency," or "trustworthiness." It speaks of integrity in both business and civic life. It is very close to the word "goodness" (v. 1), which occurs next in the same verse. Both words are two-edged and refer to social as well as spiritual matters. The first virtue depends to a large extent upon the second, since "goodness" means "a love that does not fail." This kind of love results in commitment and has, first of all, a Godward frame of reference. When one relates in a proper way to God, he will see and perform his duties toward his fellowman.

Few phrases are as complete and expressively rich as "knowledge of God" (v. 1). It means far more than a mere understanding with the mind. This knowledge is an inward feeling that God is real; it means an insight into his true nature. The central events in the life of the nation had been the events tied in closely with her deliverance from bondage. The memory of these events should have been kept alive, thus helping the people respond in a moral way to their God. To know God also meant to be aware of his power,

Ruins of an ancient Baal shrine at Baalbek in Lebanon.

glory, and moral purity. Added to this knowledge was God's purpose to redeem Israel. True worship happens when one affirms afresh his knowledge of God. Israel's problem was that her spiritual quest had become merely mechanical form and ritual. The people had thus lost a true knowledge of God. They were not concerned and did not seem aware of the nation's impending doom. They not only did not know God, they did not know that they did not know him!

Verse 2 is a vivid picture of that which had replaced virtue in the land. The five phrases are, in the Hebrew, infinitive absolutes. This verb form does not exist in the English language, but was used in the Hebrew when one wished to emphasize in a striking way the intense nature and force of the verb itself. Each of the verbs in the verse relates to God's law given at Sinai and the covenant conditioned by obedience to it. (See Deut. 5—11.) Reflected in the verbs is the fact that the land had become lawless because the people had rebelled against God's revealed will. Their sins had spilled over into every part of the nation. They had broken all the boundaries, like a river overflowing its banks. Their sin had caused a breach between man and man. The clause "blood toucheth blood" (v. 2) contains plural nouns. A violent breaking in on others for the purpose of robbery and murder is pictured. One bloody deed followed on the heels of another. The people had come to ignore even the simplest laws related to human values and decent conduct.

The Bible teaches that all God's creation suffers when man sins. A loss of man's vital powers follows, and life becomes meaningless. A wicked man drags nature down with him. This decline includes the beasts, birds, and fish. All alike share in man's well-deserved punishment. The inanimate creation of God is linked in a real way to the moral depravity of man. Modern-day ecology teaches us this truth. The Hebrew verb "mourn" (v. 3) allows either a present or future thrust. Although not fully agreed, most Old Testament interpreters relate the word to the scene of Hosea's day. The prophet may have implied future results also, but the more definite words of what would happen later occur in messages which appear later in the book.

Verse 4 forms a transition between the charges against the people in verses 1-3 and the charges against the priests in verses 5-6. What is the exact meaning of Hosea's words? Some interpreters have felt he was speaking with tongue in cheek. Others have held that he meant the people would not allow anyone to condemn their acts.

Another suggestion is that Hosea meant the people should not be condemned too much for their sin. After all, they were merely following the example set by their priests. Hosea made it clear in the verses that follow that any sin of the people was to a large extent because of their religious leaders. Roy Honeycutt says: "No people or institution is likely ever to rise higher than the quality of leadership given them. The prophets of Israel consistently focused upon leadership as the crux of the nation's ills." [2]

The Lord's statement in verse 5 mentions the prophets and another group which may be understood either as the priests or the people. Some Hebrew students suggest the word "priest" should appear in verse 5, and they translate, "O priest, thou shalt stumble." This translation is permissible. A better interpretation, however, is the possibility that God addressed the nation as a "kingdom of priests." That idea would blend better with the entire meaning of the text. Such an interpretation would agree also with the words of Moses (Ex. 19:6) to the nation as the people stood at Sinai just before the law was given.

The word "stumble" (v. 5) here refers to future punishment, not the present sin in which the priests and the prophets were walking. Hosea's oracle was prompted by the mixed worship of Baal and Jehovah at the shrine. The priests had failed to maintain the high standard of moral conduct required by Jehovah. The prophets (the word is collective) had prostituted their sacred calling for material gain. Their office had become merely a means of making a living. Isaiah (28:7) pictured them as coming in a drunken state to perform the solemn functions of their office. The words "day" and "night" (v. 5) are not merely symbols; they are literal statements of time. The prophets and priests would suffer for their sins both day and night.

The priesthood was well organized. The prophets were less well structured. The people did not look upon the prophets as having much authority. Both priests and prophets, because of their faithlessness, would stagger down into ruin. Hosea was referring to prophets who had compromised their message. Such men later would be known as false prophets. No doubt Hosea's hearers knew at once the type of prophets to whom he referred. His statement "I will destroy thy mother" (v. 5) may have referred to the nation from whom the groups came. On the other hand, he may have been referring to the priestly order or guild from whence both priests and prophets came. Institutions as well as persons are threatened by faithlessness.

2. The Lack of Spiritual Insight (*4:6-14*)

Both the source and symptoms of Israel's sins are set forth in this section. The words were addressed to the nation, but some remarks were directed to the priests. Chapter 5 contains more specific words to the religious leaders.

Rejection of Revealed Truth (4:6)

As Hosea preached, he sensed a protest from the religious leaders. They did not like his message. Therefore he sought to anticipate and answer their thoughts. The word "knowledge" is used twice in verse 6, with the definite article preceding it each time. This usage means the prophet was referring to the knowledge of God mentioned in verse 1. In a sense, he was speaking to the priests who were in charge of the law, and who were responsible for teaching the people. In another sense, though, he was speaking to Israel herself, who was intended by God to be a priestly nation (Ex. 19:6). Israel had been set apart from the heathen nations. God had spoken to her in a unique way and chosen her for his redemptive purpose. When she rejected this revealed truth, she became unusable. She placed herself on the same level with the pagan people, who were lost in the maze of false worship.

Unbridled Indulgence (4:7-13)

As the number of people grew, sin increased in Israel. As more priests were added to the religious system, corruption of the priesthood increased. The dignity and honor of the office was not confirmed by the priests' conduct. Likewise the people did not behave as they had been taught in the law. Hosea knew the priests must be stripped of their pseudo-refinement and exposed to the full light of God's moral judgment.

Verse 8 is a definite charge against the priests. They had become wealthy through unholy methods, for they had no scruples. Since they thrived on the fees paid for forgiveness, they were quite willing for the people to continue in sin so that they (the priests) could thrive on the fees paid. The phrase "like people, like priest" (v. 9) may have a double thrust in its meaning. First, people do tend to become like their spiritual leaders. Second, Hosea may have been saying that the people's punishment would come also upon the priests. The priests would not escape because of their office.

Verse 10 concerns both the priests and the people. The priests would consume the sacrifices brought to them (v. 8), but their greedy desires would not be satisfied. Reproduction meant much to the Israelites of that day. They believed children indicated God's favor. The basic theme of Hosea's preaching was that God could not approve and bless the people as long as they were engaged in the harlotry which was a part of Canaanite worship. Hosea insisted this mixing of the two religions could not assure fertility for the land. In fact, sterility would apply to land and people. James Luther Mays has written, "Israel can no more be 'my people' and worship the Baals than a wife can be married and be a prostitute." [3] The people had left the Lord and had, therefore, forfeited the blessings he delighted to send to people who obeyed him.

Those who say the Bible does not condemn social drinking of alcoholic beverages should take a good, hard look at verse 11. Many interpreters have identified verse 11 as a current wisdom saying which Hosea used to make his point. The Hebrew word rendered "whoredom" (v. 11) speaks of action without legal or moral restraint. It is the type of conduct always connected with that which debauches. No clear distinction between the two Hebrew words used in verse 11 for "wine" and "new wine" has been established. The word "understanding" renders the Hebrew of verse 11 much better than the word "heart," which appears in some versions. The Hebrew does not refer mainly to the emotions, but rather to the will and mind, which produce both affection and conduct.

A bit of sarcasm appears to be present in verse 12. The prophet pictured God as speaking of "my people," but pictured the people's crude efforts at divination from "their stock" and "their staff." We can tell much about a person's life by the way he prays. Israel had slipped into stupid ways of communicating with God, and was more influenced by pagan practices than spiritual faith.

One's spirit tells much about his whole self. It energizes his life. Hosea described his people's urge to leave the Lord as a "spirit of whoredom" (v. 12). Man's sensual nature when given free rein will destroy his spiritual grasp of things. When one's chief object in life is an inordinate desire to enjoy physical comforts and sexual pleasures, he will lose all desire for God. One of two things will happen. Either he will become a blatant atheist, or he will find a worship substitute that will not interfere with the satisfaction of his desires.

Many of the Canaanite shrines had been taken over by the Israelites for Jehovah worship. In a gradual manner, and sometimes even more quickly, the base ways of the fertility cults had found their ways into Israel's worship. The pleasant shade was good indeed! It produced a place for sacrificial meals and the sexual acts that followed. The prophet's voice rang as he condemned with bitter sarcasm the immorality that went on in Israel.

No Double Standard (4:14)
Verse 14 poses a problem in translation which affects the entire meaning of the verse. One view is that the priestesses, although guilty, did not deserve harsh treatment. The religious leaders were the ones to blame. The cultic practices, which the religious leaders condoned, had lowered the state of women in general. The men were to blame for conditions in the land. The women should not be punished while men got off free.

Another interpretation adds "the men" to the translation of verse 14, although the words are not present in the Hebrew text. They do smooth out the passage, and some translators think the words were implied. Those who omit "the men" suggest this verse means that many of the women had yielded themselves voluntarily to the disgusting sex acts in Baal worship. Moreover, the spirit of harlotry had spread from cult to town and home. God had said he would not seek to correct them through discipline. He would rather leave them to suffer the consequence of their sin in the retribution that would surely come as a result of their wicked conduct.

3. Parenthetical Message for Judah (*4:15-19*)

God's people were one even during the days of two kingdoms. Gilgal and Bethel were two of Israel's chief places of worship. Beth-aven was southeast of Bethel, but in this verse Hosea probably referred to Bethel. The word "Aven," used as the suffix to mean "wickedness" or "vanity," gives a special sting to the name. Bethel, of sacred memory in Israel's history, Hosea called "House of Wickedness." Hosea may have been influenced by Amos of the eighth century, who suggested that the people "come to Bethel, and transgress" (Amos 4:4). The clause "as Jehovah liveth" (v. 15) may have been a worship formula spoken by the people as they engaged in the disgusting practices which were a part of Baal worship. Such a statement blasphemed the name of the true God and should not have been used in such a context.

In verse 16 Hosea likened Israel to a stubborn heifer which could not be given freedom. Discipline would be applied to her. Prohibitions would be placed upon these stubborn people who had resisted every attempt to guide them. The latter part of the verse, which is probably a question, makes a new point: Since Israel had made her mind and spirit hard, could the Lord any longer give her freedom and lead her in pleasant places of abundant pasture? Freedom and privilege are for those who know how to use them.

The command "let him alone" (v. 17) was God's severe warning to Judah. Ephraim (Israel) was going down the steep cliff in a rapid manner. She would end in national ruin. Judah must not go with her. This command cannot be taken by us today as an excuse to write off some people as hopeless. That is not the point. Hosea was warning Judah not to be contaminated by Israel. The lesson is that we must guard against the influence of evil. Evil is deadly, and through familiarity we can fall under its subtle powers. God's people must love sinners, but not their sin.

4. Guilt of Israel and Her Leaders (*5:1-7*)

Chapter 5 presents a fresh start. Hosea began with direct words to those who were leaders of the nation. (This passage is part of the larger message which began at 4:1 and ends at 6:3.)

Three groups are addressed. The words "O house of Israel," "priests," and "house of the king" indicate the groups. Many Old Testament interpreters agree that the first phrase refers to those officials who were required to report to the king. They were the elders, or those who represented the people. The priests and king's household were national leaders.

The phrase "unto you pertaineth the judgment" (5:1) may mean one of two things, either of which fits the context. The prophet could have meant the responsibility for justice was theirs, or he could have meant the coming judgment would be against them in a specific way. Perhaps the prophet worded his statement so that both meanings were carried at the same time. At least one truth is clear. The prophet accused the nation's leaders of faithlessness. They should have brought justice to the people; instead they had exploited the people for personal gain.

Three towns are mentioned, along with three figures of speech from the hunter. The trap, net, and pit all were used in hunting game. The prophet scornfully accused the nation's leaders of making the people a quarry, not doing them good.

The towns named are symbolic. They call to mind times in Israel's life when the religious and political leaders had abused their offices. Because we have only meager knowledge of the facts, we cannot be sure of the meaning now. We do know, though, that the cities had one thing in common. Each contained a shrine which was closely connected with Baal worship. It may be that both were places where religious leaders had led the people into the wicked worship of a pagan cult. A third city, Shittim, is based on the Revised Standard Version text, and is not included in the King James or American Standard Versions. Most Old Testament authorities accept the RSV text as correct.

The phrase "rebuker of them all" (v. 2) suggests chastisement. The Hebrew word is used often in the context of teaching, that is, the disciplining of one's children. The people had been led astray by leaders, but the Lord was still their teacher. He would bring Israel back to himself. Even in the midst of a chapter which severely condemns sin, the redemptive and reconciling work of God shines through the prophet's stern words of reproof.

For a covenant to be valid, both parties must understand and agree to its provisions. However, more than knowing the terms of agreement is involved. Each person must know the other and know that he is known by him. Israel had lost this knowledge of the Lord, but he had not lost knowledge of them. Furthermore, Israel had lost the desire to know God. She had not sought him at the proper places and through the proper worship forms. The people were driven through the passions of their lower nature to seek a worship not consistent with the holy character of the true and living God.

Hosea stated strongly his belief that the people had no right to demur and pretend innocence before God. (See 5:3-6.) There was no hiding from God. The people were filled with a whorish spirit which dwelt within them. They had no means for self-examination, nor could they reflect objectively upon their conduct. Although they tried to find God, they could not. Their approach to him contradicted both spiritual religion and human decency. God's discipline was their prospect.

God does discipline in many ways. Violent disasters come in the processes of history, and traumatic events come to one's personal life. Ill fortune may be a way in which God is speaking to chastise and to warn. It is, though, in his silent and haunting withdrawals that he shows us our desperate need to look at ourselves afresh.

The word "treacherously" (v. 7) means "faithlessly." It was used by Jeremiah (3:20) concerning a wife and her husband. The phrase "strange children" (v. 7) refers to those who are not the offspring of a legitimate union. The awful truth was this: The people, besides turning away from God themselves, had brought into the world a generation which knew nothing of God's holy character. The latter part of verse 7 may best be rendered "now shall a month devour them." Hosea warned that Israel could be crushed at any moment. The swift invaders were poised and ready to strike. When these Assyrian hordes came, they killed and captured, and laid the land bare.

Some Jewish scholars see in the Hebrew an allusion to the month of Ab in which the Jerusalem Temple was destroyed. One should, of course, not forget that Hosea was speaking first of all to the Northern Kingdom. On the other hand, verse 5 includes Judah. Although the book contains hopeful intimations for the Southern Kingdom, we will not overlook the clear statement that "Judah also shall stumble with them" (v. 5).

As one surveys this part of the oracle, and indeed the entire unit, he sees that Israel's pride had brought her to crisis. Jeroboam II had brought wealth to the land through his conquests. The Lord was worshiped no longer. Israel looked to her own work—wealth, mansions, palaces, fortresses, and military power—for her security. Israel had turned away from God, and defied him to act in judgment.

Wicked people seldom feel any guilt as long as they are rolling in wealth and lolling in luxury. Such a land and people are doomed beyond hope. Oliver Goldsmith said,

> *Ill fares the land, to hastening ills a prey,*
> *Where wealth accumulates, and men decay.*

Such was the state in Israel, and there seemed no hope for her. The lights of opportunity had begun to flicker. In fact, it seemed they were almost out. Judgment was near. It was deserved and perhaps overdue.

5. Judgment upon Israel (*5:8-15*)

The opening of this section heralds the coming destruction. The watchman was called upon to give the danger signal. Hosea used the "cornet" and the "trumpet" (v. 8) as synonyms, although they refer to two different instruments. The first was the curved horn of a cow or ram. At an early stage in Israel's history it had been used almost always for secular purposes. It warned of things coming, or was sometimes used to announce important events. When one heard its sound, he was expected to drop his work and take his place as a fighting man. The trumpet, on the other hand, seems to have been used mainly as a sacred instrument. It was placed on Jewish coins. Pictures of it have been found in a number of religious shrines. The prophet used both of these as vehicles for his clear call for the people to prepare for God's coming in active judgment.

This section probably applies to that time when Judah came to invade the cities in the southern part of Israel. The invasion occurred soon after the Syro-Ephraimitic War in 735-734 B.C. The towns

Gibeah, Ramah, and Bethel were on the line betweeen Israel and Judah. For a number of years the two nations could not agree on whose they were. The Syro-Ephraimitic War came about when Syria and Israel made a treaty with each other against Assyria. They sought to force Judah into their pact. Judah refused. The two countries marched on Judah and captured certain cities. Judah appealed to Assyria for help. Tiglath-pileser, king of Assyria, attacked Syria and Israel. When Israel was crippled, Judah marched back on Israel and took the towns mentioned. Israel suffered attacks from both Assyria and Judah. Verse 10 makes clear that although Hosea recognized Judah as God's instrument in punishing Israel, he resented her overextending her authority or power. The landmarks (v. 10) were given divine protection (Deut. 19:14). Those who tampered with them did so in the face of divine prohibition. It is one of the lowest forms of stealing.

Verses 11-15 convey the final picture of Ephraim's doom. She had refused God's guidance and sought to find security in her own wisdom and through treaties with countries that ignored Jehovah. God was ready to act in judgment.

Three stages of God's visitation were set forth by the prophet. In verse 12 the figure of "moth" was used to portray the divine work. This is a picture of a wasting disease, or dry rot. The word is used elsewhere in the Old Testament to designate the ravages of worms. The figure speaks of a silent moral judgment constantly at work in the history of nations and men. Those who align themselves against God's eternal purposes will find their vital powers sapped away through the very actions they begin and carry out. The prophet also pictured Judah as sharing in the coming doom.

Hosea interrupted his message of doom to note that Ephraim and Judah both were aware of their need and sought help. The word "Judah" could be the understood subject of the phrase "sent to King Jareb" (v. 13). That addition would complete the parallelism of the verse and is reasonable. Often during this time both the Northern and Southern kings approached Assyria. Menahem of Israel had paid tribute to Assyria in an effort to buy her off. Ahaz, king of Judah, appealed to Assyria in a direct way, when confronted by the treaty between Syria and Ephraim. After the Syro-Ephraimitic War and its devastation of much of the Northern Kingdom in 733 B.C., King Hoshea made a treaty with Assyria.

One cannot be positive about "Jareb" in verse 13. The word may be merely a nickname for the office of Assyria's king, not the name of any one specific ruler. The Hebrew word from which this proper name is derived means "to contend" or "to strive." Some translators render the word "King Contentious" rather than Jareb.

The second stage of God's coming in judgment (v. 14) was to be more severe. The new act in this tragic drama would surpass anything the people might have believed would come. The Lord would stalk his people. All hope of escape would be futile. Like the helpless prey of the hunting lion, Israel would find herself under the power of God's punitive hand. Likewise God would make known clearly to both Israel and Judah that he is king of all the nations.

God's presence in history, though often unseen, is real. The people would see his presence in the unfolding judgment shortly to come upon them.

The third stage, though it seems the mildest, would be the most austere (v. 15). God would withdraw and leave the people in the hands of their foe. Only after they had sensed God's prolonged absence would they be willing to repent. Hosea was sure that God's absence from any real relationship to Israel would arouse the nation to her profound need. She would seek a new and vital union with her God. This would not come, however, on the front side of distress, but on its far side. Israel would suffer total defeat. Only then would she have insight to change her goals. God would wait. Time was on his side. When Israel received her share of the suffering, she would turn eagerly to God. God's purpose was clear. He wished to bring his people through judgment in order for them to see their spiritual need and return to him.

6. An Earnest Appeal for Repentance *(6:1-3)*

Some interpreters feel this section is a caricature of true repentance. However, the Greek translation of the Old Testament (the Septuagint) provides the word "saying" after "Jehovah" (v. 1). That interpretation treats the passage as real repentance and presents these verses as words spoken by the Israelites while in exile.

If one understands this passage as Hosea's message to Israel, then he reads verses 1-3 as an invitation uttered by the prophet in the name of the Lord. A person of Hosea's deep feeling could never have closed a message about judgment without urgently pleading for the people to return to the Lord. This plea may have been a song of repentance that had been used previously in times of crisis. Hosea may have used that song as a preacher today closes his sermon with a poem of invitation or a stanza from a well-known hymn.

Efforts to find mystical meanings in the two and three days (v. 2) have been many. Some interpreters say the phrase refers to the worship form of the Canaanite cults. Others believe Hosea spoke of a future millennium at Jesus' second coming. They say the two days stand for the two thousand years from the birth of Jesus until his second coming, and the third day represents the future millennium. The statement that "one day is with the Lord as a thousand years" (2 Pet. 3:8) is cited as support.

Some interpreters contend the passage is a reference to the resurrection of Jesus on the third day. Still others relate the words to an indefinite future time in which Israel would be punished, after which she would return to God in reconciliation and restoration. The reader will select that interpretation of verse 2 which corresponds best to his own understanding of Scripture.

Hosea felt Israel's root sin was a lack of knowledge (vv. 4:1; 6:3) about God. Would he not emphasize that the people should "follow on to know Jehovah"? Hosea was certain God would meet the people in mercy when they came in sorrow for their sins. As sure as the recurring cycles of nature's gracious bounty is the abundant grace of God. The Lord's kind and loving presence would be shown when the people came and confessed their sins, and professed their desire to live in the light of God's revealed will. The sorrow that had come because of sin would give way to songs of joy. If the people would renew their faith in God, he would receive them with open arms. This invitation is as modern as today's sunrise. It is the message needed for outreach in our churches today.

7. Lessons for Life from the Scriptures

Prophetic preaching is timeless. The truths voiced by a man of God apply not only to his day, but for all times and seasons. Hosea's message to Israel during her crisis has meaning for our day. Many of the things his nation faced confront us also.

Sinful living is a nation's greatest problem. Nothing will bankrupt a country in all areas of her life more than ungodly conduct. Those who are in places of leadership among the nations of the world should learn the lessons of history. A people will remain happy as long as they are related in a right way to God and his way of life. When a nation begins to ignore the moral and spiritual laws which God has written into the very structure of the universe, that nation is headed for serious trouble.

Religious leadership carries a great responsibility. Jesus said, "To whomsoever much is given, of him shall much be required" (Luke 12:48). Jesus' words are true in any realm, but especially when one assumes the task of guiding others in their spiritual lives. When one commits himself to the Lord's work in a church-related vocation, he should realize that he will have more than ordinary responsibilities. Leaders must set high standards for themselves. This is a cost of being in a place of special privilege.

Men and women both are subject to God's moral law. Obedience to God's demand for moral purity falls with equal weight upon both man and woman. When sexual looseness prevails, the woman usually suffers more. Her role in childbearing makes that fact quite probable. Jesus made it very clear, however, that there is no double standard in God's sight. (See John 8:2-11.) That which is wrong for a woman in this area is equally sinful for a man.

Human solutions cannot solve the problems resulting from rebellion against divine law. All sin is against God. The so-called social sins are, first of all, sins against the God of holiness. When we are unfair with a friend, we sin against God because God is the Creator of that person. The problems which confront our nation and our world today are present because people have not solved the matter of relating in the right way to God. Man should use all the skill he has to meet the needs that confront him in modern living. He should never forget, though, that the real solution to every need in person-to-person dealings will be found only when men become new creatures through God's grace and forgiving power.

---

[1] Oliver Goldsmith, "The Deserted Village," in *The Book of Classic English Poetry*, selected by Edwin Markham (New York: Wm. H. Wise & Co., 1934), p. 1249.

[2] Honeycutt, *op. cit.*, p. 23.

[3] From *Hosea: A Commentary*, by James Luther Mays. Published in the U.S.A. by The Westminster Press, 1969.

PERSONAL LEARNING ACTIVITIES

T F

____ ____ 1. Hosea's first sermon to Israel probably can be found in 4:1 to 6:3.

____ ____ 2. The sermon opens with a courtroom scene.

____ ____ 3. In the first part of the sermon, Hosea pictured the shame that had come on Israel and warned Judah.

____ ____ 4. Hosea then turned to Israel's national leaders: the elders, the priests, and the king's household.

____ ____ 5. Hosea concluded the message by depicting the stages of Israel's punishment.

____ ____ 6. Israel's final punishment was to be God's absence from their national life.

Answers:
1.T, 2.T, 3.T, 4.T, 5.T, 6.T.

6
"The Time Is out of Joint" [1]

HOSEA 6:4 to 8:14

Hebrew poetry is not based on rhyme, but meter. Not only meter, however, but subject matter must be taken into account. Where does one of these poems end and the other begin? We shall study these chapters in Hosea with the idea of finding a unifying theme throughout the poems and drawing helpful lessons from them.

1. Weakness of Israel's Religion (*6:4-11*)

Israel was weak and senile largely because she was shallow. Enduring loyalty to either person or cause was beyond them. Hosea began this part of his message with a double figure. First, he used a choice image—the parent faced with an unruly child. A parent who has attempted to deal with an immature, unresponsive offspring knows the frustration expressed on God's behalf. An experience from nature was the basis for Hosea's second figure. Hosea, no doubt, had observed the landscape overlaid with refreshing moisture. Quickly, however, it passed away before the rising sun.

Hosea focused upon the latter image in this passage. Israel simply lacked the depth to repent in a sincere way. As the morning cloud is brilliant with the rays of the rising sun, so Israel's shallow repentance and self-induced zeal brought promise that moral depth would come to the nation. As the early cloud dissolves in the morning sun, so Israel's brief ardor had faded before the demand for stable living and steadfast conduct.

Israel's way of life required God's action. The phrase "hewed them" (v. 5) came from the quarry. To deal with stone requires hard blows and a sharp instrument. There was, however, a two-fold function in God's dealing with his people through the prophet. God's word was to judge, but it also was to redeem.

The prophet made clear in verse 6 that God's first concern for man is that he relate himself to God properly. Hosea was not concerned merely with the structures of worship. Loving service and righteous living, rather than forms and ceremonies, declare a person's religious life sincere. Hosea's contrast of goodness with sacrifice and knowledge of God with burnt offerings was not meant to isolate two aspects of worship. He meant, rather, that when form and ceremony squeeze out spiritual worship, form and ceremony must be condemned. Religious institutions have great value, but established religious forms must never become so cherished that personal fellowship with God is placed second or ignored.

The word "Adam," which opens the passage 6:7-10, may refer to the first man of Eden. On the other hand, the Hebrew word for "mankind" is also *Adam*, and the prophet could have been speaking of the natural weakness of all men. In that case, the prophet was saying Israel had shown her human weakness as she rebelled against God.

A city named "Adam" has been located where the Jordan River was cut off while the Israelites crossed farther down the stream at Jericho (see Josh. 3:16). In verse 10 the phrase "house of Israel" could refer to Bethel. (The Hebrew word for "house" is *beth.*) These translations would mean the prophet's words refer to four cities: Adām, Gilead, Shechem, and Bethel (vv. 7-10). The sins connected with these cities stood for Israel's wicked deeds. Some students suggest the sequence of these locations pictures a pilgrim's route from Gilead to Bethel by the way of Adam and Shechem. Hosea declared strongly in the final verse in this section that the people could not avoid judgment. Bloodshed, robbery, and sexual immorality mingled with a form of worship—all these demanded that a righteous God punish the nation. Hosea reminded Judah she would share in Israel's fate (v. 11). God moved in history to judge the people for their sins. At a later time he would restore them in order that his purpose be fulfilled. The nation's skin-deep righteousness and shallow fervor would be purged through exile. The "harvest" (v. 11) meant God would remove the shallow part of Israel's life. He would replace it with a depth which would make Israel usable in the future. After her restoration to usefulness had occurred, God would work with her in his worldwide plan to redeem the nations.

2. Intensity of Israel's Wickedness (*7:1-7*)

To set apart the poems in this section and make each stand alone is not easy. The truth from one flows over into the next, and the expositor can never be certain he has divided correctly the prophet's messages. Nevertheless, we will proceed, bearing in mind the difficulties involved. Verse 1 in this poem speaks of God's desire to forgive Israel. However, God had to face the awful truth of Israel's sin and the fact that she was not willing to repent. Crime was carried on openly and without shame. Gangs of robbers lay in wait for people who were not able to defend themselves. The picture of sin in 6:8-10 is put into concise form. If one had a selfish goal, he sought to reach it through deceit. If deceit failed, brute force or even murder was the next step.

This poem describes the intense bent of Israel's sin. The people did not seem to be aware of God's holy nature. They acted as though he were a Canaanite god, not requiring that their lives and daily conduct be consistent with moral purity. God's appeal to the people, while failing to gain response, had revealed more clearly to them their guilt and shame.

The lament that Israel could not be cured is followed with a statement in verse 2 about the people's ignorance of God's method in dealing with them. Their sins had blinded them to the fact that God had a memory. However, their wicked conduct, which was rampant in the land, God could neither forget nor ignore. To some extent their blindness to the requirement of God's holiness was the root of their problem. Perhaps they knew that God was aware of their practices, but for some reason they were not gripped by the fact that God's moral judgment on sin is inevitable. Their sins had enclosed them. No escape was present from their snare. The prophet reaffirmed at the close of the verse that the Lord was not deceived about Israel's moral state.

The next five verses (7:3-7) deal with Israel's leaders and the nation's crime. The prophet spoke plainly, and made clear the fact that the people and king had made an unofficial alliance to approve of each other's wicked conduct. Their mutual corruption is described in a vivid manner. The whole nation was affected. Anarchy prevailed because there was no moral control. The king, who was a symbol of the Lord's reign in the land, should have rejoiced in righteous living and sought to promote justice. Instead, each king, while failing to punish crime, found delight in the people's lawlessness.

The word "adulterers" (7:4) refers not to Baal worshipers, but to those who were not faithful in their sex life. Hosea used a new figure of speech to describe the nation's way of life. The people in their madness and unholy passions were like a burning oven (v. 4).

Inflamed with lawless lusts, they rose to fever heat in their driving desires. The ovens of that day were round and made of burnt clay. The floor was either of stone or packed earth; the walls curved outward and took on the shape of a dome. The people were compared to the fire, not to the oven. At first the fire burned, then became smoldering ashes. The baker was busy kneading the dough and did not stop to stir up the embers and add fuel. It was the same with the people. Busy kneading out their sensual pleasures and material holdings, they had let the fires of true religion die down.

The phrase "day of our king" (v. 5) may refer to the king's birth or coronation day. The picture Hosea presented of that day (vv. 5-7) mixes drunkenness and violence. Five of Israel's last six kings were killed in cold blood. Hosea's words were spoken against the background of those years. The killings were, no doubt, related to drunken conduct. An example is Elah, a former king, who was killed by Zimri (1 Kings 16:8-14). The murder of one king and the coronation of another most likely occurred in the space of one day during the chaotic years which followed the death of Jeroboam II.

The root meaning of "adulterers" (v. 4) is "faithless." Hosea could have used the word with a double thrust, referring to those who were loose in sex and to those who were disloyal to the king. The phrase "stretched out his hand with scoffers" (v. 5) is a bit vague. Most likely, it referred to the king's association with his drinking friends or those who were conspiring in some lawless, corrupt project. The Hebrew word translated "scoffers" is used in Proverbs 20:1, where it is rendered "mocker." The picture is of lawless people who, while under the influence of strong drink, devise mischief.

The prophet resumed the picture of the oven in verses 6-7. The phrase "made ready" (v. 6) is best rendered "have brought near." The people plotted evil and looked forward to its accomplishment. The plot was kept secret as it fermented and matured. During the night it grew; in the morning the accomplished deed became known. Verse 6 is the climax to the entire picture. The expression "they are all hot as an oven" (7:7) points out that the entire group, not merely one or two, were involved in the intrigue to overthrow the kingdom. The word "judges" (v. 7) should be thought of in the broad sense of rulers, or those who measure out justice. This meaning would include the king and all those he had mustered around him to carry on the functions of government.

The last chapter of verse 7 has a note of pathos. The country had been plagued by the killing of kings, but the people did not seem at all aware of how urgent things had become. Their only hope was that God would step in quickly with divine action.

3. Inconsistency of Israel's Conduct (*7:8-16*)

This poem is a unit with two distinct sections. In the first part (vv. 8-12) the prophet pictured Israel as snatching with eager hands every chance to make treaties with the foreign nations. As a result, she imbibed their spirit more and more. In the second section (vv. 13-16) Israel's double-dealing is described, and her certain doom pronounced. The word "inconsistent" perhaps best describes the prophet's charge against the people. God had a purpose for Israel. Through her, he desired to redeem and reconcile the nations. The tragic truth, however, was that Israel was not willing to be used by God to realize this purpose.

Hosea brought three charges against Israel in verses 8-9. First, Israel had lost her identity. The prophet made that charge in the phrase "mixeth himself among the peoples" (v. 8). Israel's final years were a series of frantic experiments in political life. Seeking hard to survive, she tried to find security in treaties with other nations.

Hosea's second charge against Israel was that of unbalanced development. The figure of speech is that of a cake, most likely a pancake, burned on one side and uncooked on the other. The cake, scorched and black on one side, while steamed, damp, and lukewarm on the other, was fit only to be cast away. Many people tend to be unbalanced, concentrating on frills and fads while basic moral and spiritual matters are left unattended.

Hosea's third charge was that of unconscious decay. Verse 9 declares that strangers had devoured the strength of the nation, but the people did not realize it. "Gray hairs" (v. 9) had begun to come, but the people were not aware. They could not see their decline. One of the saddest verses in the Old Testament tells us that Samson "knew not that Jehovah was departed from him" (Judg. 16:20).

The sin for which Israel was condemned most was her pride. Pretending to be faithful to Jehovah, she ran madly to any promised security. This pretense was her doom. She either would not or could not admit that her worship was pretense, and her prayers to God were lies. This pride made her haughty. Self-delusion insulated her from self-examination. Renewal depends upon one's being honest in looking at himself, while false pride destroys. Wise men of earlier days entered pride first on the list of the seven deadly sins.

The picture of a "silly dove" (v. 11), no doubt, meant much to Hosea's hearers. In this context the word describes one who is led or misled easily. Israel could no longer reflect soberly in political matters. The people swung, like a pendulum, back and forth between Assyria and Egypt. Fluttering from one to the other, they were sending for doctors who could not heal. The basic problem, though, was not political misjudgment; it was spiritual folly. They refused to depend upon Jehovah for security. The prophets had told them over and over again they must be different because their God was different. The pagan gods were without character and, therefore, without moral constraint. But Israel and Judah were a part of God's plan to redeem the world. They must remain true to him. When they failed to be a separate people, they were guilty of foolish, even stupid, conduct. Stretching every nerve to gain power and wealth would only drag them deeper into national ruin. Their God stood with the net of a fowler, waiting to snare them as they fluttered to and fro between the great powers of the day (v. 12). Their search for help had led them into the real danger. They had left their Lord, who alone decided national destinies.

Verse 13 introduces a new thought. The people had a rebellious nature. Although God had been good to them, they had not obeyed him. They had failed to act as people who had received special blessings from God, or as people who had been chosen as a unique instrument for bringing his redemptive purpose to pass in the world. In verse 13 a threefold charge is brought against the people. They had wandered from God, trespassed against him, and spoken lies about him. This threefold treachery was based on one supreme fact. Their diplomacy was rooted in expediency rather than in confidence in the resources of a holy God. Israel's folly was that she had relied on fickle friends who had no morals or ethics. The phrase "have wandered from me" (v. 13) conveys the picture of a bird frightened out of its nest. The word for "trespass" means "rebellion" and is used in a sharp statement that reflects a violent breach of loyalty.

A bit of Hebrew parallelism is present in the latter part of verse 13. The construction lends stronger force to the pronoun, and may be rendered, "Though I, on my part, would redeem them, yet they, on their part, have spoken lies against me." Israel betrayed her God and his purpose for her to redeem his people. This offense was grave.

The "beds" (v. 14) upon which the people howled were the divans used in Baal worship. Crops had failed, but the people called upon Baal rather than Jehovah, or else they invoked Jehovah through the immoral rituals of Baal worship. The best way to translate the Hebrew rendered "assemble themselves" (v. 14) is probably "they cut themselves." This alludes to a kind of mourning that the Mosaic law forbade, although it was practiced often in Palestine. These actions were indeed a rebellion against the God of Israel.

Sometimes the best way to move people to proper living is through deeds of kindness. But with Israel even this method had failed. God had done all that he could for his people. He had taught, and he had strengthened them. What had the people done? They had rejected and even plotted evil against him. The people's treatment of God is hard to believe. They robbed the Lord of his glory by treating him as a fertility god.

The religious zeal of the people was expressed in periodic revivals of religion. Their renewal, however, was not toward higher moral standards, but toward greater sin in the name of religion. Hosea used the figure of a warped bow ("deceitful bow" v. 16), whose arrows could not reach their target. The nation's goals for solving its problems could never succeed. Israel had become a painful disappointment to Jehovah. Her fickle approach to international politics would spell doom for her leaders. The angry Assyrians would fall upon those who had guided Israel falsely. The pro-Egyptian party in Israel would receive no help from Egypt. Israel would be scorned by the very people from whom she sought help.

4. Insecurity of Israel's Position (*8:1-7*)

A trumpet blast sounded a two-fold message. Such a blast meant danger. Second, it meant authority. Both of these thrusts were present in Hosea's words. Within the realm was anarchy; without, was Assyria, ready to pounce upon the confused and flustered people. The prophet's language is terse and abrupt. Both the words and the structure of this poem were appropriate for the occasion.

The "eagle" (8:1) is a vulture. There are two Hebrew words for this type of bird. The one used here was the more hideous; it was termed an unclean animal. The bird of prey stood for terror. Doom had been decreed for the people. God was ready to punish them.

Verse 2 shows the distress the people would feel when the enemy came. Wailing and taking part in excessive ritual, they would insist they were properly related to God. Their cry, "My God," would be their way of claiming special privilege because of their heritage. Many people have this attitude. They ignore God until no other help is present, then fall back upon him. They presume upon God's grace. Yet sin has already set in motion forces which grace cannot set aside. Grace forgives sin, but grace does not suspend sin's effects. God's order is moral.

God's covenant with his people was not designed to be a despot's decree which sought blind obedience from subjects. God offered a way of life by which the people could find fulfillment. The "good" (v. 3) meant everything for which Jehovah stood. It symbolized God himself and his will for his people. The people, though, were no longer able to discern. Nothing could be done. Judgment must come.

Verses 4-6 deal with two matters causing Israel's downfall. One was the worship of idols, and the other, the disastrous choice of national goals as shown by their succession of rulers. Israel's stormy history witnessed a series of assassinations of her kings. Deceit and murder displaced kings. The people did not ask God's will for the country's ruler. Likewise the cultic ritual, which replaced pure worship, dated back to the very start of the Northern Kingdom's life. This eighth-century mixture of religions actually began with Jeroboam I, who led in worship of the golden calf and caused Israel to sin (1 Kings 12:28-30). Hosea in one sweeping indictment condemned the worship of idols and a perverted kingship. He raised the question, Is it even possible for the people to return to their former state of innocency? They seemed not able to change. Verse 6 declares idols made by human hands, such as Israel's golden calves, were not pleasing to God. They would be "broken in pieces."

Verse 7 summarizes the utter spiritual failure of Israel and its certain outcome. The figure used is a familiar one, but the form is slightly varied. Who in his right mind would try to sow the wind? Hosea must have had his tongue in cheek as he thought of a man plowing the soil carefully, harrowing it, then planting wind instead of seed. What kind of crop would come from such folly? He then recalled the wreck and ruin of a Palestinian hurricane. He proclaimed that when the divine ledger was reckoned, Israel's sins would cause a harvest like a destroying blast. Nothing but ruin would be left in its pathway. Should there be an occasional sprout or growth, there would be no yield of food. He even suggested a most unlikely event: Should some food abide, foreigners would quickly devour it.

Israel's idol worship and immorality was the direct cause of the nation's fate. Israel had chosen to defy God and break her covenant with him. Now she had to pay for it.

5. Foolishness of Israel's Activities (*8:8-14*)

Verse 8 begins a new poem. There may be significance, however, in the fact that the word "swallow" is present in the last verse of the preceding poem and in the first verse of this one. Quite often when poems were gathered and arranged, a key phrase or a kindred thought was used as a connecting link.

Israel had behaved in a foolish manner. Her uniqueness was gone because of her self-will. She had sought to satisfy sensual desires in worship, and national safety in foreign alliances. As a result, the nation would fall shortly. In fact, the crumbling process had already begun. These words of Hosea, delivered after 733 B.C., probably were spoken shortly before Samaria fell in 722 B.C. Large parts of the Northern Kingdom had been captured already and made an Assyrian province. The straw was in the wind.

The phrase a "vessel wherein none delighteth" (v. 8) has a double meaning. It may describe a thing lovely to look at, but more properly, a tool employed to perform a task. Israel's sin placed her on the same level with the other nations locked in a power struggle for life itself. She had been chosen to occupy a unique place in God's purpose to redeem the world. When she chose to forfeit that privilege, she became neither fancy nor useful. Her haughty air would deepen her shame when God's judgment upon her was completed.

The "now" of verse 8 and "are gone" of verse 9 show both sin and judgment were in process at the same time. "Wild ass" (v. 9) is a pun in the Hebrew, being very much like the word "Ephraim." Israel had gone to seek a mate. Having taken pagan customs, the people found more in common with foreigners than with the few Hebrews still faithful to God. The Hebrew of verse 9 may be rendered, "Ephraim hath given love gifts." The reference is to Israel's attempt to gain help from foreign nations, chiefly Assyria and Egypt. During her hectic last days, she went first to one and then to the other in a mad effort to survive. Israel's folly, as shown by her wild schemes, soon would be made evident. The Hebrew word translated "gather" (v. 10) means "punish." One cannot buy friendship. When he attempts to do so, he finds only despair. God would bring Israel's foolish plans to a tragic end.

The phrase "king of princes" (v. 10) is not found elsewhere in the Old Testament. It may be rendered "king of kings," a title which Tiglath-pileser claimed for himself. More likely, however, the term was related to the boast of the Assyrian king in Isaiah 10:8, "Are not my princes all of them kings?" Israel had been foolish in her foreign policy. Her negotiations with Assyria had not produced safety from the threat of invasion. Her attempt to purchase goodwill rather had become a cause of both the decline and the ultimate eclipse of the kingdom.

God's plan was for Israel to have one altar—the place which the Lord chose (Deut. 12:5). Wisdom rested in such a command. Worship became corrupt because of the many altars (8:11) which the people had built. The root problem, of course, was not the number of altars, but the type of worship carried on at those altars. Unholy rites prevailed, since the worship was Baal oriented. When crisis came, the number of sacrifices increased. No effort, however, was made by the people to clean up their personal lives. Altars built to deal with guilt became a place for the breeding of greater guilt. Rather than having brought the people to a personal encounter with the Lord, the altars made the breach even wider.

Israel's problem was not a failure to know God's will. The people had been taught thoroughly. The "ten thousand things of my law" (8:12) translates a Hebrew word which means "abundance" or "fullness." In the Mosaic laws, oral traditions, and words from the prophets, Israel had been given enough teaching to make her without excuse. God's way of life should have been constantly a part of her consciousness. She had ignored the moral precepts and had chosen a ritual without value. That was her sin.

The first phrase in 8:13 is paralleled by the second. The people offered sacrifices to the Lord, but ignored the offering's deeper meaning. That which mattered most was the dinner with meat, not the experience of God's forgiveness. The worship service should have focused on God's demands for righteous living, but it became a time for gluttony and excess. The altars became the springheads for many sins. God could not accept such foolish conduct. It only called to his mind the sin and hypocrisy of the people who still called themselves his people. He must punish them. If he failed to do so, he would be inconsistent with his own holiness.

The phrase "shall return to Egypt" (8:13) may have meant that Egypt would invade Israel. On the other hand, the phrase may have been a poetic expression for exile in general. The people should have grasped this reference easily, since God had brought them up out of bondage in Egypt many years before Hosea spoke. One may accept either meaning and remain true to the spirit of Hosea's message.

Verse 14 gives a graphic statement of the nation's foolish actions. First, Israel had her mind on material things. Second, she had come to depend upon herself. The word rendered "temples" (8:14) in the King James Version should, no doubt, be rendered "palaces," as in the American Standard Version. The word denotes large and splendid buildings.

Man never remains without activity. If he rejects actions based in righteousness, he will do the opposite. Jeremiah (2:13) spoke at a later time of the two evils the people had committed. He said, "They have forsaken me, the fountain of living waters, and hewed them out cisterns, broken cisterns, that can hold no water."

Hosea stated that Israel had built palaces, while Judah had "multiplied fortified cities" (8:14). God's judgment would fall on the buildings and cities alike. Proud self-exaltation would turn to shame when the Lord's righteous wrath brought doom to the land. The picture of judgment by fire (see 8:14) was a current figure of speech. Amos used it seven times (1:4 to 2:5) as he described the judgment that would come upon Israel and the nearby nations.

These five poems presented a dark picture for Israel. There seemed little, if any, hope for the nation. Hosea must have delivered his message with a broken heart. Shakespeare's Hamlet voiced the feeling that must have gripped the prophet:

> *The time is out of joint: O cursed spite,*
> *That ever I was born to set it right!*

6. Lessons for Life from the Scriptures

Hosea's poignant pleadings speak across the centuries. Human nature has not changed. That which pleased God in Hosea's day brings delight to him now. That which broke his heart and stirred his wrath in ancient Israel does the same today.

Shallow righteousness produces no permanent spiritual result. Changing moods and inconstant resolves always have been one of religion's chief problems. To serve God requires that we have more than mere emotion. We need the power available for living by clear principles and demonstrating integrity. This power comes from a life-changing experience with the Lord.

False concepts of God lead to immoral living. To the ancient Jew, God had revealed himself through the law given to his covenant people. To Christians, Jesus is the fullness of God's revelation. God's self-revelation both in the law and in Christ levies a moral demand upon men and women. To turn from that revelation is to invite lowered moral demands, immoral living, and the sure judgment which follows.

Man needs to develop his total personality, not merely a part of it. Too many people emphasize one aspect of the Christian life and ignore other areas. Some are enthusiastic about eschatology (doctrine of last things), but neglect ethics. Some stress evangelism, but say little about Christian nurture. Some contend strongly for personal piety, but have no place in their program for social responsibility. These unbalanced emphases impose upon Christianity unnecessary strain on its credibility with the lost. Full-grown spiritual maturity means a balanced Christian life, and a balanced presentation of Christianity to the world.

---

[1] William Shakespeare, "Hamlet, Prince of Denmark," I,v,189-190, in *Great Books of the Western World*, ed. William George Clark and William Aldis Wright, Vol. 27 (Chicago: Encyclopaedia Britannica, Inc., 1952), p. 39.

PERSONAL LEARNING ACTIVITIES

1. The author uses a series of words in the chapter subheads to describe Israel's condition. Match the words in the two columns according to the author's description of Israel as found in those subheads:

____ Weakness	1. Conduct
____ Intensity	2. Activities
____ Inconsistency	3. Religion
____ Insecurity	4. Position
____ Foolishness	5. Wickedness

2. The author describes this passage as a series of __________ based on __________ and __________ __________.

Answers:
1. 3,5,1,4,2; 2. *poems, meter, subject matter.*

7
"Doom Beyond the Saddest Guess"[1]

HOSEA 9:1 to 10:15

Hosea's words in this section continue the gloomy picture painted in the previous poems. We cannot be certain about the dates of each unit. All of them reflect the background of the last years of the Northern Kingdom. The units within this section become more intense as they move along, and it may be that each one in turn is slightly nearer the time of Israel's complete collapse.

1. Depth of Israel's Guilt (*9:1-9*)

There are many smaller thoughts within this unit, but there is no reason to divide it into fragments. The nine-verse passage has a theme. Each thought supports and adds to the other. A solemn climax is reached in the last verse. In the first section (vv. 1-3) the prophet uttered a stern word about the revelry of the people on a feast day. He then warned them about the certain exile that awaited them. They would not at that time be able to worship because they would be ritually unclean. Their food and drink would be polluted as a result of their being on foreign soil. The section closes with a strong statement about the nearness of the judgment hour and an observation of the people's attitude toward the prophets. Hosea brought the oracle to an end by a comparison of Israel's present sin with her deep corruption at Gibeah. The God of history could not and would not allow such guilt to remain unpunished.

The feasts of the ancient Israelites were times of joy and mirth. They were in many ways like our national holidays. The autumn feast called *Sukkoth* was a time of special delight. A rich harvest spoke of God's favor upon the people. Abundant crops and fruitful vines called for jubilant celebration and thanksgiving, which often ended in undisciplined orgies.

Hosea crashed into one of these festive occasions. He abruptly stopped the people and told them they had no cause to rejoice. Their present affair would be their last. By the time of the next annual feast the sanctuary would lie silent. No one would be there. Weeds instead of worshipers would be present.

In the first verse the literal Hebrew says, "Rejoice not, Israel, to exult." This second verb has within it the idea of loud and noisy laughter. Standing in contrast to the common words for praise, it calls to mind the worship of the Canaanites. Rather than a rejoicing in the mighty acts of God, the verb "exult" suggests a shallow glee at the magic techniques of the Canaanite fertility ritual.

Hosea pictured Israel's defection from God under the sign of a harlot (v. 1). In the picture also was Israel's actual conduct in Canaanite worship. Interpreters are divided as to the exact meaning of the latter part of verse 1. Some feel it speaks of sex acts on the grain floors, while others contend the prophet had in mind greed for material things.

The basic point, however, is clear. The people were giving credit to Baal for the blessings sent by Jehovah. Unbridled indulgence had replaced holiness. At the very moment the foundations of Israel's national structure were crumbling, the people were going deeper into sin.

Such a condition could not continue. The prophet named two places of captivity (Egypt and Assyria). This matter has been dealt with in the preceding chapter. Assyria was of course the nation that crushed Israel and carried her into exile. Hosea was not wrong, however, when he spoke of Egypt also in connection with the coming judgment. Symbolically, Egypt stood for bondage. Also small groups did migrate at different times into Egypt, sometimes voluntarily and sometimes as captives. More than a century later, in the days of Jeremiah, a large group from the Southern Kingdom took abode in Egypt. We need to remember that Hosea's message was not confined to the Northern Kingdom. Quite often he spoke in a direct way to Judah.

The wine offerings, or drink offerings (v. 4), went along with the burnt offering. The pouring out of wine pointed out the joy which came to one whose sins God had forgiven. In stating that the Israelites could not present wine offerings, Hosea was saying that joy in God's forgiveness would cease. Their gifts would not be pleasing nor even welcome. Thus the people would no longer have the means prescribed for making peace with God. The bread of mourners refers to food eaten during the time the people were grieving for a dead person. The Jews had strong feelings about the impurity of a person who was in any way connected with a corpse. He was ritually unclean and therefore could not take part in any religious act—especially one which dealt with getting forgiveness from God.

Hosea declared that in exile the food which in normal times was brought into God's house for the purpose of worship would only be used to satisfy the physical needs of the people. No sanctuary would be in the foreign land, and its absence would have an adverse effect against any true worship. Hosea never forgot the fact justice was more important than forms of worship. But he still gave proper place to institutions in the nation's religious life. To him worship could not be entirely valid in a foreign land because no sanctuaries of Jehovah would be present.

Hosea's threats about the future contained a striking note of irony. Under the Baal forms of worship the people had eaten food as gluttons. They forgot the Lord and sought only to quench their physical hunger. When the judgment came, matters would be reversed. They would not be able to bring sacrifices into God's house. Only the hunger of their bodies would be satisfied; their spiritual yearnings would be unmet. Sin often pays off in strange ways.

What greater distress can come to a nation than to lose the right to worship? Hosea's cutting question in verse 5 was the deathblow to the people. Exile would make worship rites impossible. What would the people do when the day came for the next autumn feast? The treatment received in the foreign countries would surely teach them that their present worship had been nothing but corrupt blasphemy against the covenant God. The phrase "pleasant things of silver" (v. 6) may refer to the vessels which they used in lawful and proper worship. The phrase, however, reminds us of the words in 8:4 which refer to the idols they had made. The nettles and thorns (v. 6) speak in a striking way of the final series of events leading to Israel's doom. Shrines to Baal, once crowded with people, would be left deserted. The word "tents" (v. 6) may refer to the idol-tents of the high places (Ezek. 16:16), or perhaps to their own dwelling places (2 Sam. 20:1). Memphis was the capital of Lower Egypt and a city of great importance. Hosea used that city to stand for the entire kingdom of Egypt.

The last segment of this poem (vv. 7-9) sets forth the nearest thing in the book to an account of the people's response to Hosea's preaching. The words, however, are tantalizingly brief and not fully clear. The section opens with a picture of judgment as having occurred

(v. 7). The prophet took for granted the nation had received her due reward for sin. The word "visitation" in this context means "punishment," and thus stands side by side with "recompense." The statements are in the past tense and most likely should be thought of as having occurred. This form is used in Hebrew when the prophet was so sure something was going to come to pass that he spoke of it as though it had already occurred. Historically, the exile had begun. Assyria's having taken some of the Israelites captive in 733 B.C. served as a foretaste of the nation's coming doom. The clause "Israel shall know it" (v. 7) was thus in the process of being fulfilled. Later the knowledge would be complete.

The words about the prophet in verse 7 may refer to the false prophet who had promised peace and wealth for the land. Hosea said that the false prophet would be shown up as a fool. Or the words about the prophet may have been the people's response to Hosea's message. In this view the people dismissed the man of God with scorn. They assumed an air of super wisdom and saw Hosea as one in the state of frenzy, thus one on whose message they could not depend. Hosea argued that the people thought of the prophet as foolish and mad because they were blinded to the truth by their sinful conduct. Their wicked lives produced an enmity which had clouded sober thinking and mature evaluation.

Further evidence of the people's bitter spirit and bias against God's prophet is the picture of Ephraim as "a watchman with my God" (v. 8). The Hebrew text is not easy at this point, but the thought seems to be that the sinful people chose to trap the prophet, not support him. They lay in wait, seeking every chance to catch him in some mistake in order to discount his message. The fact that Hosea used the first person pronoun "my" in speaking of God should present no problem. Quite often the prophet so identified himself with God that he found himself switching personal pronouns, thus bringing out the closeness he felt for his God. This most likely was a spontaneous action on the prophet's part and reflected his intense nearness to Jehovah.

When the prophet referred to Gibeah (v. 9) in the same breath as the people's guilt, he made a striking point. Few times in the Scriptures is sin described in such an intense way. The prophet referred to the shameful story in Judges 19—21. The account describes an awful crime against the Levite and his concubine. As a result of the crime, almost the entire tribe of Benjamin was slaughtered. The prophet made his point clearly. Israel's sin was deep. She had no moral sensitivity; her guilt was compounded. God must punish her. Judgment would not be merely in the distant future, but was an immediate reality. The day of payment had already begun to dawn, and its forward tread could not be halted. Death for some and captivity for others would be the harvest of the seed the nation had sown.

2. Briefness of Israel's Glory (*9:10-17*)

Hosea must have spoken with a touch of nostalgia when he mentioned Israel's early years. As he thought of the woodland walks of his boyhood days, he may have called to mind a vine filled with luscious blue grapes—the kind which grew in large amounts in certain places about the highlands in Ephraim. These were grapes like Caleb and Joshua found on their trip as spies throughout the land (Num. 13:1-33). Hosea saw that his early years and those of Israel's had much in common. Surprise and joy greeted Israel's beginning as a nation. God set forth much promise for this group of slaves, even though at the first they lacked both order and charm. What was it Israel had at the start and her neighbors lacked? Was it not an insight into godly things? Whether or not this was the reason, God did choose her as the channel through which his redemptive program would be worked out. Through them he would bring the sinful world back to himself.

All was different now. Israel's glory had departed. With the swiftness of the bird's flight, Israel's status and honor among the nations was gone. The "first-ripe in the fig-tree" (v. 10) was always a delight to the eye. Likewise Israel was special to God. When she failed to measure up to the hope of the one who chose her, and trampled her chances for greatness under foot, she sank to an even lower level than the pagan people.

When did the failure begin? Hosea traced Israel's revolt against God to an event which occurred even before the nation entered the Promised Land (see Num. 25:1-3). The first generation beyond the Exodus yielded to the sexual rites which went along with the cultic worship of the Moabites. Although the avowed purpose was to secure the promise of a rich harvest, a side payment also occurred. The Canaanite worship had great appeal to the lustful nature of the people. Hosea described their conduct as a "shameful thing" (v. 10). He contended that the way of life they began to love was loathsome in God's sight.

Translators do not agree on how the first part of verse 13 should be rendered. Most of them translate it so that Ephraim is compared with Tyre, in which were blended beauty and strength. Later, pride became her curse and downfall. Likewise Israel, blessed of God, set in a pleasant place and firmly rooted, had become a victim of that pride which deprives of grace. Some Bible interpreters, however, contend that the Hebrew text does not refer to Tyre, but to the Israelite men who were destined to be a prey in battle. Whatever the meaning, the basic thought in the Hebrew is still the same. Israel had sinned and had thus exposed her sons to pursuit and slaughter. If the Israelites mustered for war, they would end up facing massacre.

The phrase in the first part of verse 14 has been called a rhetorical question. The prophet used the words in a skillful way. He produced the effect of a question while giving a graphic picture of alarm. The thought conveyed is that as the prophet started to pray for some type of mercy, he broke in upon his own prayer with a new thought. Since the nation was doomed, the kindest thing God could do for the people would be to make them no longer able to bring forth children.

What had the people done in Gilgal to move Jehovah to reject them and to decree in Hosea's day that they must be expulsed from the land (v. 15)? Saul was crowned by the people as king at Gilgal. Hosea recalled this act was against God's ideal will for them. Jehovah wished to choose their leaders rather than bind them to a king and kingdom based on flesh and blood. He wished for Israel to be unique, and not like the nations roundabout them. Hosea may have felt the people's desire for a kingdom was one of their chief sins against God.

Also one of the nation's centers of idol worship was Gilgal. No proof exists that it was the chief place for human sacrifice, but there are many evidences that rites of Baal worship were performed there.

The word "hated" (v. 15) is used in a special sense. We know from the New Testament that God does not hate people, only their sin. (See 1 Tim. 2:3-4; 2 Pet. 3:9.) W. R. Harper in *The International Critical Commentary* speaks of the phrase "will love them no more" as an "anthropomorphic expression for the decision to withdraw all favor and mercy from Israel." [2]

The clause "their princes are revolters" (v. 15) is a play on words in the Hebrew. George Adam Smith renders it, "All their nobles are rebels." [3] Box suggests, "All their rulers are unruly." [4] Horton renders it, "All their princes are prancers." [5] The Hebrew word translated "revolters," which described the princes or leaders, is used in 4:16, where Israel is pictured as a "stubborn heifer." Hosea laid the blame of Israel squarely upon her incompetent and wicked leaders.

The direct words of God end with verse 16. The nation's root had been destroyed. No hope was held out for further growth. The prophet suddenly left the realm of the abstract to utter a concrete statement. If any children were brought forth, they would be killed quickly.

The prophet himself made a final statement in the last verse. He said "my God" (v. 17) because it was no longer proper to call Jehovah Israel's God. The people had turned down God and his claim upon their lives. On the other hand, Jehovah was Hosea's God. Hosea had been called to be God's spokesman. The prophet thus set himself as opposed to his own people.

The appeal of the prophet had fallen upon deaf ears. This section, however, does not close with a threat that the people would be destroyed. Rather, they were to be banished. Room is thus left for them to be restored. The Hebrew prophet never conceived of God's giving up completely. Sinful man might delay God's program, but nothing could prevent God's final purpose.

3. The Disappearance of Israel's Institutions (*10:1-8*)

In this poem Hosea repeated much of what he had said in some of his early sermons. One concern, however, is present in a striking way. The institutions which had been a part of Israel's life were doomed. Israel's course, which she had chosen herself, had paved the way for the doom of the system which had been a part of her life. These institutions were the altars, worship rites, shrines, symbols, and leaders—including the kings.

Israel had become an affluent nation. Although scholars do not agree on the best way to translate it, the word "luxuriant" (10:1) is best understood as the vine to which Israel is compared. Israel was a religious nation. As her riches grew, her religious impulses grew also. Israel's religious life prospered as the good things came to her. The problem, however, was that Israel's carnal nature shaped her religious practices. She made cultic altars to the pagan religions, not to Jehovah worship. Israel was not concerned with a just social order. Neither did she seek to build a noble moral life. She rather gave way to the lustful nature which lay within her depraved heart. The phrase "heart is divided" (v. 2) refers not to lack of ability to decide, but to the merging of religious systems. Some of the phrases from Jehovah worship may have been present, but the basic format was cultic. It was filled with sex and loose morals. Some translators render this phrase as "heart is smooth," which would speak of a certain suave approach on the part of these worldly-wise people as they worshiped.

The word "now" occurs in both 2,3. It speaks of the urgency of Israel's crisis. It was God who would "smite their altars" (v. 2) and "destroy their pillars" (v. 2)—both of which items were related to their worship. The word "smite" means "break the neck of," and is used elsewhere in the Old Testament for breaking the neck of an animal. The altars could refer, of course, to the horns or calves' heads at the corners of the altars. In the first clause, "he" is emphatic in the Hebrew. The translation may be rendered, "He, himself, will smite the altars."

The people had lost their respect for their leaders, since the citizens no longer depended upon their kings. Some interpreters believe the phrase "have no king" (v. 3) shows that this message was brought after the death of Pekah, and before Hoshea was chosen as the one to succeed him. Whether or not this interpretation is true, Hosea clearly implied a distinct relationship between the people's concept of God and their king. In their conceit they felt the need for neither.

Israel's failure to be consistent in worship showed itself in her language. She had no integrity. She made treaties with foreign nations, but planned to observe them only as long as she could reap benefits. The clause "judgment springeth up as hemlock" (v. 4) does not refer to a punitive action from God. Rather, it speaks of how right had decayed into wrong and had spread as weeds throughout the land.

The coming judgment is pictured in verses 5-6. Assyria's attack upon Israel would cause great grief. Israel's sorrow, however, would be wrongly motivated. The people would grieve because they had lost their loathsome worship, not because they had been guilty of doing wrong. The corrupt leaders had exchanged the glory of Jehovah for a shallow religion that appealed to the people's lower nature.

Any prestige connected with the calves used in worship would fade away when judgment fell upon the land. Hosea called Bethel (House of God) Beth-aven (House of vanity). (See v. 5.) Bethel was the place where Jacob first met God. Later, however, Jeroboam I had made it a place for a rival altar to compete with Jerusalem. Later still, it became a center of Baal worship. The prophet might have been using the name Beth-aven to refer symbolically to all the Baal worship in Israel.

Israel would suffer a double shame in connection with her religious calves. First, they would have no power to aid her when the foe came. Second, they would be carried away and placed in the trophy room of the Assyrian king. This custom of taking a nation's gods as spoil showed that the victory was really a conquest over the gods of one's opponent. Shame would come to Israel when the idols ended up in a parade on the way to the Assyrian court. Two things would be made clear. First, Bethel's bull was useless. Second, it was foolish. Baal worship would be exposed to disgrace and set forth before the Israelites as a fraud without power. No matter how much the people implored, the symbols to Baal's power could not be a source of strength to Israel.

The picture in verse 7 refers to the kingly office, rather than a specific king. The nation's monarchs had been unable to move in a straight path. The short, hectic reigns during the last days of Israel were both a cause and a reflection of the nation's failure to remain stable. Israel is pictured as a bubble on the surface of the water. The thought is of something which is light, empty, and worthless. Israel was driven by the torrents of international intrigue. The nation, drained of its strength, was swept quickly away by the flood that broke in from Assyria.

The final verse in this section (v. 8) combines a summary of the coming doom with a prayer which the prophet put into the mouth of the people. Aven stands for Bethel, which was on a hill. (Hosea always related the high places to Israel's sin.) The altars of Aven would be torn down. Wild brambles would cover the altars. In this pronouncement we can feel the outraged disgust of Hosea over the people's sin. He added to this prophecy a picture of the hopeless despair of the people as they stood in awe and terror before the wrath of God. Helpless because their false gods had failed them, the deceived people would be filled with dismay. They had lavished their love and praise upon the cultic objects rather than upon the Lord. Their fate would be to pray for death. They had turned down the God of holiness. Their institutions as well as their identity would come to a tragic end.

4. Stubbornness of Israel's Rebellion (*10:9-11*)

As Hosea's life and work came nearer to Israel's fall, he dealt more with events of the past. He sought to make clear Israel's crisis by looking back on her history. The awful conduct of Israel at Gibeah has been discussed (Hos. 9:9; Judg. 19—21). Both the deed itself and the action that followed, foul and carnal in every way, showed the lewdness and folly of the people. Hosea maintained that through the years Israel had kept up her breach of faith in God and his commands. The people had defied God and trusted themselves as much in the prophet's day as they had during the early years of their life as a nation. Some students contend Hosea referred to Gibeah because it was Saul's home. They see in this passage an allusion to the starting of the kingdom at the death of Samuel. Even as Israel had sinned when she demanded a king, so she had stayed a rebel nation during the reign of every monarch from Jeroboam I to Hoshea. Israel, in wanting an earthly ruler, was seeking to maintain her own future in the marketplace of international politics. She showed a lack of faith in God and his power to raise up righteous leaders in the time of Israel's crises.

The clause "there they stood" (v. 9) should be rendered "there have they continued." This description, no doubt, referred to the people's evil choices through the centuries. The judgment is true whether the prophet was looking back to the days of the judges or to the crowning of Saul as king.

The latter part of verse 9 is not easy to translate. Some modern versions have taken great liberty with the text. There are, however, two ways of bringing the Hebrew into English, either of which fits the context well. One is to say that such a terrible slaughter as occurred during the period of the judges had not yet come to Israel. When God decreed, such bloodshed could come again. The other is based on the fact that Gibeah is located in the most southern part of the Northern Kingdom. When the judgment came to Israel, it would reach even as far as this last outpost. Gibeah would not escape because she was in a remote part of the country.

Verse 10 makes plain that Israel's fate was in God's plan. His punitive action would be coordinated with external public history. To Hosea, Jehovah was Lord of world history and used the nations as his agents according to his own judgment. Israel had lessons to learn. Although Judah is not mentioned here in a special way, she is by no means ignored. God had chosen his people as agents of his redemptive work. Chastisement must come to Israel in order that in the years to come she might be used in an effective way to accomplish his purpose. How much she would suffer in order to be made ready for her mission was God's verdict and his alone. The clause "peoples shall be gathered against them" (v. 10) may be a veiled reference to the gathering of the other tribes against Benjamin at Gibeah. They nearly destroyed this small tribe because of her grievous sin.

The phrase "bound to their two transgressions" (v. 10) is of uncertain meaning. Many students think that the double iniquity was the outrage at Gibeah and the people's awful sin in Hosea's day. However, the two sins may have been when the people rejected the house of David as the true king at Solomon's death and when they embraced Baal as a god worthy of worship.

Hosea's last figure of speech in this section was taken from his early homelife on the farm. In the early days in Ephraim, cows were used often to thresh. This work did not involve a heavy yoke, but rather walking over the grain in the threshing circle in a leisurely way. The young heifer was left without a muzzle. She could eat as she worked (Deut. 25:4). Loving her job, she grew fat and sleek. Things were pleasant, productive, and profitable. This reference is an idealized picture of Israel's life and her nearness to the Lord in the early years of her history.

As the years passed, however, the nation forgot God and failed to remain grateful. No longer eager to follow the wishes of her Master, Israel became lawless. The land was filled with a lack of justice. The early spirit of eagerness to learn and obey changed to one of loving that which was false and doing that which was wicked. God was forced to come in judgment. Ephraim would not be treated as a petted heifer any longer. A yoke would be put on her neck. It would rub and chafe. The harder work of plowing and harrowing would replace the joyous privilege of threshing. The phrase "have passed over upon her fair neck" (v. 11) suggests that whereas the people had been spared hard slavery, they were about to face it in the soon coming exile. The phrase "will set a rider on Ephraim" (v. 11) expresses the idea of a heavy yoke upon the neck. This yoke was used for drawing and driving. The images "shall plow" (v. 11) and "shall break his clods" (v. 11) picture hard labor in the field. The hard labor, of course, stands for subjugation and bondage.

To be certain about the use of the terms "Ephraim," "Judah," and "Jacob" is not easy. Most likely, these terms present a form of parallelism. One great truth, however, is contained in this passage. Both the Northern and Southern Kingdoms would suffer when the foe came. The poem ends with a picture of the severity of judgment, which was certain and would be soon.

5. Necessity for Israel's Repentance (*10:12-15*)

In this last poem the prophet for a moment changed his tone. He exhorted and invited. The hour was not too late for Israel to repent and escape the coming judgment. Hosea seemed, however, to sense that his appeal was useless. Israel had gone too far, he thought. She had come to love that which was wicked and hate that which was righteous. Finding godly things distasteful, the people had come to love nothing save that which appealed to the lusts of their lower nature. The brief word urging Israel to repent is followed quickly by a firm statement. Israel's failure to be grateful and remain faithful to God moved the prophet to pour out his wrath upon them.

The first three verbs in verse 12 are all imperatives. It may be, however, that the first two should be bound together with a conditional force. In that case, the prophet would be saying, "If you will sow righteousness, you may reap mercy." In other words, if the people would repent even at this late hour, God could and would forgive them and remove the coming judgment upon the land. A moral miracle could still take place. If Israel would come forth with an earnest resolve to follow God, the doom which had been pictured in graphic terms could yet be averted. The fallow ground refers to virgin soil. The people were called upon to make arable the land which had not yet been sown. This figure of speech shows the people must change their course of conduct. They must commence a new course of life, give up old habits, and find joy in serving God. This is an Old Testament picture of New Testament repentance.

If the people were to turn over to God the hard and weed-infested soil of their sinful hearts, they would experience God's grace. The promise to "rain righteousness" (v. 12) means that God's grace would destroy the seeds of sin in a thorough manner. God's blessings would not spring up from good deeds which had been sown, but be rained down as grace from heaven. Here is a picture of Christ our righteousness sent down from heaven as a full measure of God's reconciling grace.

Verse 13, however, seems to negate any chance that Israel would repent. The bitter contrast between that which God looked for and found is set forth. The divine purpose has been thwarted by human deeds. The phrases "have plowed wickedness" (v. 13) and "have reaped iniquity" (v. 13) both denote completed action. Of course, the reaping was in process. There would, however, be an even larger fulfillment. The Hebrew word translated "lies" (v. 13) has within it the idea of disappointment. This translation suits the context in an ideal way. The people had put their trust in human strength and skill. Not content to find their safety in a holy God, they wanted religious results without spiritual discipline. They felt a great army would assure them both wealth and freedom, and give them both prestige and the power of free choice.

How wrong they were! The power Israel trusted would be the power that brought her down. She thought her safety was through treaties with foreign powers—a contradiction of everything God had taught through his prophets. Foreign powers were God's means of judgment.

Hosea speaks of Shalman and Bethel-arbel (v. 14). Most likely, the reference is to the killing of Zechariah by Shallum (2 Kings 15:10). However, it could be to the campaign of Shalmaneser against Samaria and the nearby lands in 722 B.C. Beth-arbel was near Gilead and was the scene of a vicious mass murder of children at a previous time. The coming catastrophe for Israel would be in some respects like this unforgettable massacre of the past.

In verse 15 the prophet was personifying Israel's sin by his use of the word "Beth-el." The awful judgment which was coming to the land had been caused by those sinful deeds which centered in Bethel. He therefore spoke of Beth-el as the cause of the coming ruin. The phrase "at daybreak" (v. 15) most likely speaks of the speed with which Israel's monarch would fall. As one awakes and finds a new day has dawned, so Israel in a sudden moment would find her kingdom had gone. Some interpreters, however, contend the word "daybreak" refers to the wealth of the land. If so, the prophet was saying that adversity would come when the nation least looked for it. The word "king" may refer to Hoshea, Israel's last ruler. More likely, however, it refers to the kingship as a whole. The Northern Kingdom, which had begun as a rebel movement and was maintained by constant defection from God's will, would come to a tragic end.

John Greenleaf Whittier was speaking of mankind's basic problem, but he described Israel's in Hosea's day when he said,

Oh, doom beyond the saddest guess,
As the long years of God unroll,
To make thy dreary selfishness
The prison of a soul!

6. Lessons for Life from the Scriptures

The darker the sky, the clearer the stars shine. Israel was in her midnight hour. Yet out of this moral and spiritual darkness certain lessons for life emerge.

A nation should consult God when choosing leaders. Our country is not a kingdom with a family succession. We have a choice. We elect our leaders. Each person should be aware that his own vote is a priceless treasure. He should learn the facts about those running for office and seek God's will when he casts his vote.

Those things we substitute for the true God never bring us a happy

life. The biggest disappointments we shall ever have are those that come to us as we search for a happy life through the things the world offers. Many years ago a poet said,

But pleasures are like poppies spread,
You seize the flower, its bloom is shed;
Or, like the snow falls in the river,
A moment white—then melts for ever.[6]

If we go on turning our backs upon God, we soon lose both the desire and the capacity for godly things. Although the door is always open to God's love, we can reject his pleadings so many times they cease to attract us. We are then no longer sensitive to his calling, and we are color-blind in the moral realm. God does not cease to woo, but we place ourselves outside hearing distance.

When we fail to be aware of our blessings and rebel against God's will, he must chastise us. God uses this process so that we may be drawn closer to him. We thus become more usable, and God can work out his purposes through us.

God's grace is always present. Even if matters seem hopeless, God will step in and deliver his people when they show a sincere desire to do his will. The basic fact of God's nature is that he is willing and even eager to forgive his people and restore them to his living presence.

---

[1] John Greenleaf Whittier, "The Answer" in *The Complete Poetical Works of John Greenleaf Whittier* (Boston: Houghton Mifflin Company, 1894), p. 441.

[2] W. R. Harper, *The International Critical Commentary,* Amos and Hosea (Edinburgh: T. & T. Clark, 1953), p. 339.

[3] Smith, *op. cit.,* p. 307.

[4] George Arthur Buttrick, commentary editor, *The Interpreter's Bible,* Vol. 6 (Nashville: Abingdon Press, 1956), p. 667.

[5] *Ibid.*

[6] Robert Burns, "Tam o' Shanter. A Tale," in *The Book of Classic English Poetry,* selected by Edwin Markham (New York: Wm. H. Wise & Co., 1934), p. 1330.

PERSONAL LEARNING ACTIVITIES

1. According to the author, Hosea 9:1 to 10:15 probably relates primarily to ______ (1) Israel's early history; ______ (2) Israel's last years.

2. Hosea 9:7 may indicate the people's response to Hosea's message. If so, they said (check one): ______ (1) "The prophet is right." ______ (2) "The prophet is a fool." ______ (3) "The prophet is sincere." Relate your response to attitudes you have observed toward modern-day pastors.
3. Judgment would come to Israel through war's ravages as inflicted by __________.

Answers:

1. (2); 2. (2), *your answer;* 3. *Assyria.*

8
Love's Labor Is Never Lost [1]

HOSEA 11:1-11

God's righteous character must never become a screen obscuring his love. Even more, we must never convey through our teaching or preaching that God's love is so holy it cannot abide the presence of sinners. Without meaning to, we can insist so much on righteous living that we conceal the tender mercy and wondrous grace of our Creator and Redeemer.

Perhaps Hosea had this in mind when he placed between two sections condemning Israel's sin one of the most heartwarming poems on the Father's love to be found in all literature. The fact that God's love is pictured elsewhere in the book under the figure of a husband pleading for his bride should in no way cause us to reject this figure of the father who loves the wayward son. One figure of speech cannot exhaust all the spiritual truth about our heavenly Father. Hosea's basic concept of God was not judge or king, but parent.

In bringing this picture to the people, the prophet reduced the tension between two great facts—God's mercy and his wrath. To the critic, these facts may seem to refute each other. But in the parent both mercy and discipline are present within the context of love.

1. God's Elective Love *(11:1)*

Many people find the doctrine of election hard to accept. In the Old Testament, however, it is simple and uncomplicated. God chose people for the service they could render. God's purpose to redeem the world was rooted in his nature and revealed in his work. He chose a slave people without any merit of which they could boast as the means by which he would bring his purpose to pass.

God's love for Israel is the romance of the ages. He did not choose Egypt with her years of wisdom and culture nor Assyria with her military might. God chose a slave people to be his son; he called a child to be his hope for the future. When he brought Israel from the womb of chaos and bondage and set her under the guidance of the Law (which was given at Sinai), he acted as creatively as when he ordered light to come out of darkness.

The word rendered "child" (11:1) can be used for a mere infant or for an adolescent. In fact, this same word is used to describe Joshua (Ex. 33:11) when he was forty-five years old. The context makes clear, however, that here God was speaking of the tender years of Israel's life. This verse parallels in a striking way the passage in Matthew (2:15) where the exodus of the infant Jesus after a brief sojourn in Egypt is spoken of as that which fulfilled these words of Hosea.

Hosea did not create the concept of Israel as God's son. When Moses stood before the burning bush (Ex. 4:22-23), Jehovah spoke of Israel as "my son" and "my first-born." Although Israel was weak and helpless because of the Egyptian oppression, God loved his child and resolved to bring him from the affliction of the iron furnace. Israel was indeed unformed as long as the people were in Egypt. The call came to them in order to establish a relationship. This calling is one of the meanings of election. Likewise the idea in the word translated "son" is that of helpless dependence upon an adult. The word translated "loved" (11:1) expresses a point of beginning—"I began to love him." Contained in the word is a biblical motif which grows throughout the Old Testament and reaches its climax in the Word become flesh. Hosea's tender recollection of events foreshadowed the winsome message of the gospel. For the prophet's words to be echoed in the early words of Matthew is natural to biblical thought.

2. God's Constant Disappointment (*11:2*)

One can almost feel the lump in Hosea's throat after his first statement. The child who had been blessed refused to change and respond to the kindness of his loving father. Although the prophet spoke of Israel's failure in only a few words, he spoke with deep feeling.

God's first call was by no means the only one that came to his people. In every period of Israel's life the divine message came afresh. Israel was often reminded of her unique mission. Every kindness bestowed upon Israel was in one sense a repeat of the original call. God was seeking always to make his relationship to his people a thing of the present, not merely the past. Each new effort put forth by him through the centuries, however, had been rebuffed. Israel seemed to be more and more determined to be a rebel son.

At first glance, Hosea's statements in 11:2 do not appear to agree with the thought in chapter 2. In the figure of Israel as bride the prophet conceived of a time when the youth was faithful. Can these two figures be reconciled?

When did Israel's folly begin? Hosea claimed (9:10) it was in the loathsome worship at Baal-peor found in Numbers 25. Hosea also referred to unholy conduct at Gilead (6:7-8), Shechem (6:9), Gilgal (9:15), and Gibeah (10:9). Here, however, Hosea seemed to equate the first calling and the first sinning. Perhaps he did not mean to refer to isolated events. Perhaps his statement here should be looked upon as a concise summary of Israel's entire history. When viewed as a whole, the nation's complete life-style was that of Baal worship and conduct based upon it. Hosea was dealing in concepts rather than concrete facts. As he looked upon it, Israel's response to the divine call was to refuse God from the very start. That which had become outward in recent days had been inward from the first. Although Israel was a pure bride during her desert honeymoon, she was from the first already a woman of the world. She gave response to her groom to begin the marriage, but her heart was never in it. Unless there had been some fragment of bridal love, the union could never have been consummated. In a shallow sense Israel became a religious nation. She had enough semblance of obedience to set up a framework of intimacy with God. But Israel never committed herself to the Lord with perfect love. She was both a rebel bride and rebel son from the outset.

Was God's labor of love entirely lost? Not at all. A small group within the nation remained faithful to him. Ideas developed and in due time bore fruit. One of God's goals was to prepare Israel to accept the doctrine of monotheism once and for all. This verse, taken apart from the context of Israel's life, does not tell the complete story. Even though Israel became absorbed in the cultic worship of Baal, her basic ties with God were not wholly dissolved. God was working with his people. His resources were great enough to defeat all those things which caused Israel to depart from him and adopt a pagan way of life. Israel did defect at times, and this wandering delayed God's program and brought him sorrow. He would not, however, give up in his resolve to redeem the nations through Israel, whom he had chosen.

3. God's Wise Guidance (*11:3-4*)

One of the truest marks of greatness is tolerance of a weaker person. Patient kindness and tender care are Godlike qualities.

The first phrase of verse 3 stands in direct contrast to the terms "Baalim" and "graven images" of verse 2. In the Hebrew the verse begins with the first person pronoun. This construct gives the idea extra emphasis. A proper translation would be, "I, on my part, taught Ephraim to walk." Whereas the false gods were without power to aid the people, Jehovah had the resources and the desire to lead the infant nation in a tender way. Their first faltering steps, when weakness and insecurity threatened, were taken with God's help. The picture of a parent's leading a child to put firm steps on the ground for the first time always is heart stirring. Jehovah guided Israel in a loving way. He never became tired of her little attempts to walk. Long before the people could reason for themselves, God through his prophets pointed out the path with loving and winsome words.

The parental picture of verse 3 is a lovely climax to Hosea's message. The Lord did more than guide the tottering infant's footsteps. When the child became tired, Jehovah carried him in tender arms. Until the infant learned to walk well, the Lord watched over him to assure his safety. G.A.F. Knight renders it, "Yet it was I who taught my little son to take his first steps. If he fell and hurt his knees, it was I, his Father, who kissed him better." [2]

One of Hosea's choice figures was that of healing (5:13; 6:1; 7:1). He may have had in mind especially the time when God told Moses to place the brazen serpent on the pole so that those persons bitten by fiery snakes could be restored to health (Num. 21:4-9). Many times throughout the Old Testament God's purpose and program to redeem and save his people is pictured under the figure of healing.

Although God's love carried the people through crises they were not able to meet in their own strength, they refused to acknowledge their dependence upon God. Their blindness, no doubt, was due to their stubborn nature. None are so blind as those who refuse to see. Israel's sin was not lack of knowledge, but lack of humility. She refused to acknowledge God's goodness and grace. Ingratitude has been described many ways, but William Shakespeare came as close to Hosea's meaning as any writer when he caused one of his characters to say,

How sharper than a serpent's tooth it is
To have a thankless child! [3]

Although the basic thought remains the same, a new figure of speech is employed in verse 4. The prophet changes the picture of Israel from a small infant to a team of bullocks presided over by a kind driver. This image stands in contrast with the unruly heifer in Hosea 10:11. The phrase "cords of a man" suggests God used kindly discipline, the discipline which takes into account man's dignity and frailty. God's humane treatment quieted the people's fears, assured their doubts, and gave strength where they were weak. The discipline was done within the context of that love which only God can give. Hosea was convinced that if Israel ever gave herself to God, it would be on the basis of God's loving presence, not his thunderous threats.

Bible interpreters do not agree on how the phrase "lift up the yoke on their jaws" should be rendered. Some translators prefer "as they that lift an infant to their cheek," rather than "lift up the yoke on their jaws." However, the language probably pictures a yoke placed carefully upon the neck and jaws. Israel was to feel no undue pressure; her obedience to God was to be voluntary.

The phrase "laid food before them" gives the symbol more meaning. George Adam Smith pictures the heifers toiling up a steep road.[4] There was no need for rough ropes to keep the frisky animals at their work. By the gentle touch at the mouth and sympathetic words in their ears, the heifers were drawn on. The driver eased the yoke to prevent its pressing and rubbing against the beast. He then rested and fed the animals when they reached the top of the hill. Even so did God draw Israel on toward the fulfillment of his purpose.

4. God's Stern Chastisement (*11:5-7*)

Every wise parent knows the child will require discipline sometimes. This poem on God's love does not ignore the present tragic state in Israel. When a people who have been blessed refuse to respond in a proper way, conflict results. Many human fathers whose sons have rebelled against them have thought complete abandonment was the only answer. If loving-kindness is met with shameful ingratitude, some type of judgment must occur. In his former messages he had recited them in detail, but always to no avail. In this message he merely contrasted the past and future. As the people heard the message, they were to apply it. Each would know himself the cause of the crisis that was facing the nation.

Although translations of the clause "they shall not return into the land of Egypt" (v. 5) vary, this writer accepts the reading of the American Standard Version. When the first clause of the verse is read thus, the contrast with the latter part of the verse is clear. The prophet was saying that the people would suffer a far more severe punishment from Assyria than they had suffered from Egypt before the Exodus. When the Assyrians came upon them, their lives would be hopeless. The type of warfare carried on by Tiglath-pileser and those who followed him was, beyond doubt, the cruelest the world had known up to that time.

Verse 6 describes in a graphic way how Israel would be destroyed. The sword was a symbol for the destructive power of war, since it was the main weapon used in conflict. The word rendered "bars" stood for poles or cross beams with which the city's gates were fastened. Some interpreters have translated it "branches" instead of "bars," thus making it a symbol for the mighty men of Israel. This latter translation is more likely correct.

Whatever the exact meaning of the word, the thought is clear. The people had been wise in their own eyes and had sought to live without God. Thus God had decreed they must be destroyed. There was no escape. The God whom they refused to serve and whose counsels they refused to heed would not be present to protect them when the foe came.

The phrase "bent on backsliding" (v. 7) may be rendered "are hung to it." This word picture still has meaning in our day. When we are hung to a thing, we may sway to and fro within certain limits, but within those limits we cannot be moved. In other words, we have a power of motion, but it has certain limits. Likewise Israel still had a certain amount of mobility, but she was restrained within the hand of God's purpose. She had adopted a life-style which was not in keeping with God's holy nature and his purpose for the nation. The prophets had urged the people to be a part of God's plan to redeem the world, but the pleadings were useless. Israel's way of life had become raging and reckless. The people would be dealt with. Since they wished to be free from God, he would leave them alone; they would be on their own.

Man can suffer no more awful fate than God's withdrawal. Paul's haunting words "God gave them up" (Rom. 1:24) fits the fate of Hosea's people. The dreadful suffering they experienced at Assyria's hand is history. That suffering was one result of God's absence from their lives.

5. God's Recoiling Agony (*11:8*)

At this point the whole tone of the poem changes. God's warnings ceased. He must now decide. Israel deserved the full and fierce flame of his anger. She had not been grateful; she had rebelled. Thus she deserved no mercy. The time had arrived for drastic action.

The opening statements in verse 8 are not questions. Rather, they are exclamations. One way we can know God's feelings is through human terms. Here God's sorrow is expressed in the human terms of mingled emotions. Yet God is just. Can he still be a God of great mercy? These two qualities are both a part of his person; one does not thwart nor make void the other. A wrath is present in his love, and a love is present in his wrath.

The prophet's questions went like this: Should God allow the seeds of evil to ripen into a harvest of utter ruin? Or should he intervene? What could he do as a last resort? His holy nature demanded that his people be holy. However, his love shrank from the prospect of their destruction. Were the two facts—human sin and divine love—in hopeless conflict?

To the Hebrew, the heart was the seat of feeling as well as conscious action and will. Hosea pictured God's love as taking a hostile stand against Israel's complete doom. The Lord could not bear the prospect of Ephraim's destruction. The phrase rendered "turned within me" (v. 8) has the idea of the heart being acted upon; it conveys the idea of a sincere change. Although God had decreed judgment against Israel in the form of complete ruin, mercy spoke and prevailed. The tenderness of the Father's love overcame the severe verdict of the Judge's sentence. The clause "compassions are kindled together" (v. 8) speaks of sympathy as a rill from the full flowing stream of God's amazing grace. This same verb is used to describe Joseph's feelings toward his brother Benjamin (Gen. 43:30). The Scripture is rendered, "His heart yearned over his brother." Those who translate "My compassion grows warm and tender" (RSV) do a good job. The text thus rendered conveys both the heat and the glow of God's steadfast love for Israel and his overshadowing presence that refused to give her up.

6. God's Dramatic Decision (*11:9*)

One must weigh the facts, but a time comes to act. When the time arrived for God to act, he was equal to the occasion. Hosea pointed out that God's grace transcended Israel's guilt, and compelled him to spare her from complete oblivion. However, God did not revoke his decree to punish the people. He sent them into exile, but with the hope of return. Thus the sin was to be punished, but the nation was not to be destroyed.

What was the basis of God's decision? God does not act as a

man because God is not man. His being other than man is the root meaning of the word "holy." Since God is other than man, he must act in a way that is true to his nature. No simple answer to this question can be found or expressed. We never quite answer it until we see the "Word become flesh" dwell among us and go to the cross for our sins. (See John 1:1-5,9-14.) In Jesus we see justice and mercy blended into a love which redeems and makes all things new. Christ knew no sin, and yet he was made to become sin that we might be made righteous. In the Old Testament God said, "I am God, not man"; in Jesus Christ, God says, "I am both God and man." God's last word to man is not a message of doom, but of salvation.

7. God's Loving Prayer (*11:10-11*)

Once again the scene quickly changes. The prophet pictured God as no longer in debate with himself about Israel's fate. The nation had gone through tragic ruin. The people were scattered. A new exodus was about to take place. God's purpose to create and redeem had been kindled afresh. The time to reject Israel was gone. A new time had arrived—a day to receive her anew. The people who had been cast off were to return and become once more and finally the people of God.

Those interpreters who contend these last two verses are non-Hoseanic simply do not see the real message of the chapter. Hosea nowhere maintained Israel would escape doom. She had sinned, and sin must be dealt with. To withhold judgment would have been contrary to God's moral nature. The point was, however, that Israel would not be destroyed. When God had chastised his people and worked out his purpose through this act, his mercy would show itself. The exiles would be gathered home.

The prophet did not go into detail about how God would restore Israel. He was more concerned with the result. He pictured the people in verses 10-11 as having been made pure through their sorrow, and thus ready to follow the Lord. The phrase "walk after Jehovah" (v. 10) shows their ready response to his purpose for them. When the signal came, they would find joy as they followed the Lord in faith and humbly served the God who had refused to give them up.

The picture of a roaring lion in verse 10 stands in contrast to the figure used in 5:14 and 13:7. There the roar is a sign of judgment. The picture in this verse is that of a father calling the young lions. The "trembling" (v. 10) suggests the awe of respect and the joy of anticipation. The prodigal children would come in both fear and hope.

What about the sections from which they come? The "west" (v. 10) speaks of the islands of the Mediterranean Sea or the coastlands. Egypt, of course, stands for the south. Assyria may denote both north and east, since the exiles who returned from Babylon were forced to circle the desert and come to Israel from the north. Thus all four directions are set forth in this picture of the people's return.

Although the Northern Kingdom went into the Assyrian exile, many individuals went at other times into other areas. Quite a few went to Egypt. Babylon conquered Assyria in 605 B.C., and, no doubt, carried the captive Israelites to her land. There they were joined later by the captives from the Southern Kingdom, which fell to Babylon in three stages—605 B.C., 597 B.C., 586 B.C. The book of Ezra makes plain the fact that the return from Babylon included people from all twelve tribes.

In verse 11 Hosea used the image of a "bird" (sparrow) and a "dove" to picture the exiles in their homeward journey. Two figures are present. We see, first of all, swiftness. Also suggested by the "trembling" used in verses 10,11 is the thrill of people eager to return home. The former image of "stupidity" or "folly" pictured by the dove (7:11) is not present in this figure of speech. The entire message is that of the awesome delight and rapid manner with which the people would respond to the Lord's call.

Many Bible interpreters see in Hosea's words more than the restoration of a remnant. They believe he spoke of God's people in all places being brought back to him. In other words, they relate this prophecy, not merely to Israel after the Exile, but to spiritual Israel—God's great worldwide kingdom. Their interpretation is that when the Lord would "roar," men would come from all four corners of the world. The people would tremble as they repented of their sins and would rejoice greatly as they heard the good tidings about life in Jesus Christ. Pusey, who is fond of finding pictures which others often miss, connects the phrase "roar like a lion" with Jesus Christ who is the Lion of the tribe of Judah. Pusey says: "His *roaring* is His loud call to repentance, by Himself and by His Apostles. The voice of God to sinners, although full of love, must be full of awe too. He calls them, not only to flee to His mercy, but to *flee from the wrath to come.* He shall call to them with a voice of Majesty and command." [5]

There are other Bible interpreters who see in Hosea's words more than a return from Babylonian Exile. They see a prediction of national Israel's being brought back to her homeland in the days just before the glorious second appearing of Jesus Christ. These scholars say the Jews will come from every part of the world, as these two verses state.

What is the real message of this passage? Bible students will never be in complete accord concerning the future of national Israel. One great truth, however, must be received by all who know Jesus Christ as Savior and Lord. God's love will win the victory. Love's labor will never be lost. Although temporary setbacks may delay God's cause, they cannot destroy it. God called Israel to be his people through whom he would redeem the world. Many times along the way she failed to accept her mission. His love, however, never ceased wooing her. In God's time Jesus Christ came through his chosen people. National Israel turned Jesus down, but God called a nucleus who became the seed for the Christian kingdom. Christianity today bears witness that God has won the victory through his unfailing love. In all places where men serve Jesus, witness is borne to the truth spoken by Hosea many years ago.

8. Lessons for Life from the Scriptures

Few passages in the Bible reveal the depth of God's love with such insight. In our day the true nature of love has become twisted. It is thus refreshing to find an ancient writing with such meaning and relevance to the needs of our modern world.

When God calls, he guides. Election should never be looked upon in a merely static sense. It is dynamically charged with certainties because of God's unfailing resources. God's power is linked with his love. The one who began a good work in us will go on leading and molding until his purpose is complete. He will sustain our steps, direct our walk, and lift us up when we fall down. He will deal gently, kindly, and with tender care. He may chide, but he will never forsake.

Man's failure to be grateful is, first of all, a spiritual problem. God's great love places a strong duty upon man. If he despises this love and refuses to respond with a thankful life, he is guilty of the greatest sin of all. One of the major reasons for our lack of peace among men is there are so many little spirits among us. They need the transforming touch of God's power, which saves, redeems, and causes one to live the grateful life.

Cruelty drives, but love draws. An old truism says, "No cord or cable can draw so forcibly, or bind so fast, as love can do with only a silken thread." Men cannot be driven like dumb cattle. They must be treated with respect. We are human beings, not machines.

Love is that which can transform ambition into selfless service, greed into gratitude, and getting into giving. When love prevails, we cease to be people who demand. We choose, rather, to be like Christ, who gave himself for others. Cruelty, like the winter wind, only freezes us and makes us stubborn. Love, on the other hand, like the warm sunshine, melts us. We no longer resist God's will, but serve gladly the one who inspires us through his own love and kindness.

True love refuses to despair. Someone has said that love is blind. This statement is doubtful. Love is the most keen-eyed emotion among us. If you want to know a man's defects, ask his wife. The only sense in which love is blind is that it on purpose shuts its eyes to the defects of the one loved. Love centers its purpose and focuses its aim on what the other person can be, rather than on what he is. Only in this way can one be delivered from a moral weakness. Love refuses to give up, but goes on having faith in the person. Love will not quit believing until the ideal has become reality.

No person can completely fathom the depth of God's mercy. Human beings love as human beings. God loves as God. The reason we shall never know the depth and mystery of the cross is that we lack knowledge. We never have loved anyone at such a great cost. We never have sacrificed to forgive as God did when he gave his Son as a ransom for the sinful world.

I stand amazed in the presence
Of Jesus the Nazarene,
And wonder how He could love me,
A sinner, condemned, unclean.[6]

Only those who love know ultimate victory. The world is structured in such a way that the last battle can never be won by evil. Neither can cruelty be the best way by which people are led to act. Those who live for others are the ones who know the joy of inward peace. We are not made sweet by taking the acid fluids out, but by experiencing Christ's love within. That love mellows, purifies, and transforms our desires. Through love we learn how to reconcile, mend, repair, and create anew our dealings with both friends and enemies. Love is a pebble which when dropped into the pool of life can send ripples to the farthest shores. Those who know love know the meaning of fulfilled lives and true joy.

---

[1] The title of this chapter is a variation of the title of a play by Shakespeare, "Love's Labour's Lost," *op. cit.*, Vol. 26, p. 254.
[2] G.A.F. Knight, *Hosea* (London: SCM Press, 1960), p. 109.
[3] Shakespeare, "King Lear," I,iv,310-11, *op. cit.*, Vol. 27, p. 253.
[4] Smith, *op. cit.*, p. 320.
[5] Pusey, *op. cit.*, p. 115.
[6] Charles H. Gabriel, "I Stand Amazed in the Presence," *Baptist Hymnal*, *op. cit.*, p. 63.

PERSONAL LEARNING ACTIVITIES

1. Hosea began chapter 11 by reference to Israel as (select one): ____ (1) wife, ____ (2) daughter, ____ (3) son.
2. Hosea 11:8 pictures God's dilemma, which may be described as his (God's) being pulled upon by both (select one set): ____ (1) joy and sadness, ____ (2) anger and neglect, ____ (3) justice and mercy.
3. God resolved his own dilemma in verse 10 by (select one): ____ (1) decreeing Israel's destruction, ____ (2) ignoring Israel's sin, ____ (3) purposing to preserve Israel through judgment.

Answers:
1. (3); 2. (3); 3. (3).

9
"How Long May Men Go On in Sin?" [1]

HOSEA 11:12 to 13:16

This passage has been called Hosea's final argument. The people were about to take a leap into oblivion. Hosea had one last message for them—an appeal to history. They were urged to learn a lesson by looking at Israel's past and thinking upon her relationship with God through the years.

To be certain about the literary structure of all the material in these chapters is not easy. No doubt exists, however, that the last verse in chapter 11 should go with chapters 12—13. In the Hebrew text the last verse of chapter 11 is the first verse of chapter 12. No point of theology is involved, and many people today accept this arrangement as correct.

Is this entire passage one unit? Is it a single message brought by the prophet? Good reasons for taking that position may be found. On the other hand, some interpreters divide the passage into two sections (11:12 to 12:14; 13:1-16). Still others see the passage as a group of smaller poems like the material in 6:4 to 10:15. This writer contends we should view the passage as one entire unit, although he suggests that fresh starts are taken in 12:2; 12:7; 13:1; 13:9; and 13:15.

A word should be said about the text of these two chapters. Most readers do not know Hebrew. When they compare English versions, they become confused. Sometimes the readings not only vary, but say the exact opposite. These variant readings can be explained by the difficulty of the Hebrew text. Many Bible translators have edited the text to make a smooth translation. As we have observed, the most popular and well-respected versions vary greatly. This study will not attempt to reconcile these differences. We shall accept the traditional English text and interpret that text in the light of facts known about Hosea's time and tongue.

A quick summary of the overall contents of these chapters will serve as a basis for an in-depth study. Thematic unity is present, whether the passage is considered one oracle or several. The once strong people have been sapped by prosperity. Now they are forgetful and stupid. They do not seem able to realize how urgent things have become. Sins have become ripe for judgment. The time is late in Israel's history, but perhaps not too late. (Every true prophet of God keeps on hoping—even until the midnight hour arrives.)

In the first two verses (11:12 to 12:1) Hosea drew a contrast between the two kingdoms' loyalty to Jehovah. These verses precede a charge against Judah (12:2-6), a charge which is cast in the form of a lawsuit. They may be viewed either as a separate oracle or as prelude to the larger section.

A new start is definitely begun in 12:7. Whether it is part of a larger discourse or not is irrelevant to the message. Ephraim is pictured as a Canaanite—the trader holding rigged scales—who boasts of economic success. An announcement from God follows. The nation would be punished and dwell, as Jacob did in the early days of his austerity, in tents. No reason exists for excluding verses 11-14 as a part of this message. Verses 11-12 focus upon the nation's sin. (See the statements against Gilead and Gilgal.) An event which appears to tie this passage closely to 12:2-6 came from Jacob's life. Notice that the reference to Jacob occurs several times. The last two verses of this section (vv. 13-14) remind the nation of the prophet's important role in Israel's life, and describe Ephraim's bitter future. The people's wicked deeds have provoked the Lord to anger.

The entire chapter 13 is a sober picture of Judah's state. No word of hope is in it unless one interprets verse 14 as a gleam of promise. (See the later discussion.) The shadows deepen with the passing of each statement. The last two verses of the chapter leave no doubt about Israel's fate. The details are not given, but the figure of speech suggests tragedy. The people will be torn into pieces and devoured in the cruelest manner. The nation will disappear into nothingness. The physical pain will be shocking. The entire passage ends in a gloom and darkness illuminated only by the prophet's own sturdy belief in the final goodness of God.

1. Ephraim's Deceit and Judah's Faithfulness
(11:12 to 12:1)

These two verses may be viewed as a distinct message. They introduce

A modern Bible land scene of men harvesting in the ancient manner.

Hosea's last bitter word against the nation (12:2 to 13:16) before the final call to repent (14:1-9). The Lord spoke, not merely the prophet. Every place God looked he found people who practiced double-dealing and falsehood. The idea is that sin was so prevalent God could see nothing else. Although the people had exploited their neighbors, they ultimately had practiced falsehood and deceit against the Lord. Later (v. 7) the prophet emphasized how the people exploited their fellowmen.

The Israelites' first and chief lie was their calf worship. This practice meant all their worship forms, even their repentance and prayers, were one great falsehood. The pretense underlay, penetrated, and corrupted their entire way of life. They were not, of course, fooling God. They were, rather, kidding themselves. They thought the Holy One of Israel could be bribed with this type of worship.

Hosea's side-glances toward Judah are interesting. His message was mainly to the Northern Kingdom, but he was aware of the Southern Kingdom too. For Hosea to have spoken to Israel, but to have said nothing to her sister to the south would have been strange indeed. This passage (11:12 to 12:1) presents Hosea as God's spokesman to both Israel and Judah.

As one consults the various versions today, he is inclined to throw up his hands and quit. They not only differ; they say very different things. The older versions for the most part speak well of Judah. She was still faithful even though Israel had rebelled. Many of the modern versions, however, insist that Judah, like Israel, had forsaken God.

Why the difference? The problem is not one of the text, but of context. A literal translation is, "But Judah still walks with God, and with the Holy One is faithful." The word "walks," however, could be translated "wanders," "rolls," or "runs about." Thus the Hebrew could mean, "Judah is still wandering about, but is faithful to the Holy One." This translation paves the way for Hosea's charge against Judah in 12:2.

The best way to translate "feedeth on" (12:1) probably is "herds." The verse pictures Ephraim as a shepherd or hunter. She spends her time, however, in herding wind, not flocks, and in hunting the sirocco, or deadly southeast wind, rather than game. This metaphor combines two ideas—emptiness and destructiveness. Wind suggests that which is empty and elusive. The fearful sirocco blew from the desert and was accompanied by piles of sand. It brought suffering, anguish, and even death to both man and beast. Ephraim ran after that which was not only insubstantial, but harmful. This parching and withering wind destroyed vegetation, and came in its whirling force as the blighting breath of ruin. This picture describes well Ephraim's political activity—void, empty, useless, and fatal.

Israel refused to take a firm stand in her political life. She showed she was not stable. The covenant with God was not enough. She added to it by courting Egypt's favor through gifts. Olive oil was one of Palestine's chief and most precious natural products. Hosea used oil to represent all the wealth which Israel poured into Egypt to secure her help. Ephraim's policy—empty like the wind—was evidence of her spiritual bankruptcy. She relied on things which, although they seemed good, were destined to produce ultimate ruin. The nation had placed her trust in lying words, acts of deceit, and vain fancies. Often when people are nearing physical starvation, they find themselves no longer able to appreciate good food. Something like this had happened to Ephraim. She was no longer able to appreciate the good. Her taste for that which was righteous and good was gone.

2. An Indictment with Lessons from History
(*12:2-6*)

The format of this section is a courtroom scene. Hosea was bringing a legal suit for the Lord against Judah. Verse 2 contains a parallelism with both Judah and Jacob the defendant. We cannot be certain: Is Jacob synonymous with Judah? If not, then Jacob refers to Israel and thus includes both parts of the divided kingdom. More likely, Jacob and Judah were meant to be the same. Hosea named them both as a quick reference to the days of the patriarchs, and thus he used the nation's past to bring the present under judgment. We may note in passing that this allusion to events that happened before the Exodus is the first in Hosea's preaching.

The prophet did not mean to suggest Israel inherited the guilt of her forefathers. Hosea was no fatalist. The people made the choice themselves with their own free will. They were, however, following directly in the footsteps of the ambitious and tricky Jacob. Although outward things had changed, Judah and Jacob's conduct were very much alike.

Hosea stressed three events in his reference to Jacob. First, Jacob had hold of Esau's heel when he came forth from the womb (Gen. 25:26). Second, the clause "in his manhood he had power with God" (v. 3) most likely refers to the first clause in verse 4, which concerns his struggle with the angel (Gen. 32:24-29). The third clause, "he found him at Bethel" (v. 4), refers to the same event, but explains further. As a result of his struggle with the angel, Jacob's name was changed to Israel. His name change meant a heart change.

Interpreters have viewed these events in different ways. Was God praising or blaming Jacob for seizing his brother's heel? Most likely, Hosea was saying Jacob began his career in manipulation. When he became older, he tried to manipulate God. In the wrestling match, however, he learned physical strength and mental agility do not suffice for spiritual blessings. He was forced to plead with God in order to become a man of integrity. In the clause "he found him at Bethel" this subject is debated. Did Jacob or God do the finding? One point is clear, though, whichever side we take. The clause "there he spake with us" (v. 4) expresses a timeless truth. Any person who strives with God and yields to him is transformed. He then shall find the will and purpose of God for his life.

Jacob is a unique person in the Old Testament. He was a rascal in every sense of the word. He cheated, connived, and manipulated for personal gain. Yet God saw something good in him. He chose Jacob rather than Esau as the channel through whom the Savior would come. God's action was a message to Hosea's Israel and Judah. The truth is for us also. No matter how sinful one may be, God can change him. Then God can use this person as he by faith seeks God's will for his life.

One's name comes to stand for his character. This truism applied in a special way to Israel's God. When God's name was mentioned, all the associations of history came before the mind of the Israelite. Jehovah was not a tribal god. Neither was he a part of the cultic worship of the Canaanites. He was the Self-existing One. His name stood for redemption. He had revealed himself by name to Moses. The name stood for moral character, ethical principles, mercy, and forgiveness. All these meanings were a part of Hosea's phrase, "Jehovah, the God of hosts" (v. 5). Hosea's name for God referred also to God's power to protect. In symbol he was the leader of Israel's armies. Verse 5 is a transition. The prophet was about to invite the people, if not command them, to repent.

How was Israel to turn to her Lord? She must do more than repent in a shallow manner. Moral and ethical demands always are a part of Jehovah's gracious call. Hosea gave a two-fold injunction. Justice must be blended with kindness in Israel's dealings with man. Also the people must show complete trust in God. The word rendered "kindness" (v. 6) is a difficult word to translate from the Hebrew. No English word catches its true meaning. Among the words suggested are "love," "piety," and "devotion." "Kindness" includes attitudes and actions which create and maintain a relationship. This relationship can come by birth, the social order, or through an arrangement. One shows this quality when he is concerned with and responds to a person and his need. This need is always met within a framework of relationship. One of the tenderest words in the Hebrew language, it is also one of the most expressive. The fact that Israel was sincere in turning to God would be shown by her willingness to relate to others. She would reveal rightness and fairness in her daily life and render justice to all classes of people. One may deceive himself about his way of relating to God. He may even rationalize when he deals with his inward feelings. However, he cannot deny the way he treats his neighbor. Hosea suggested that man's relationship to God is mirrored in his relationship to his fellowman.

The final aspect in Hosea's call to repentance concerns man's willingness to trust God for deliverance. The penitent must "wait . . . continually" (v. 6). This kind of waiting implies a patient hope and complete trust in God in all life's crises.

3. Israel's Materialism and God's Answer
(*12:7-14*)

This section begins in a startling manner. Hosea hurled sharp abuse at Israel. She is called "a trafficker" (v. 7), a word that has been rendered also "Canaanite," "merchant," and "swindler." God meant for Israel to be a wholesome influence on the other nations. Instead, the people had imbibed the pagan spirit, then expressed it both in their idol worship and business tactics. The term "Canaan" means "lowland," and was applied to all lowlands of Palestine, including Phoenicia. The Phoenicians were merchants noted for their sharp dealings. Thus Hosea's charge was a severe rebuke expressed with stinging sarcasm.

Hosea spoke of the nation as a person who sought to defend herself because of her wealth. She claimed in a blatant way that she had done nothing wrong in gaining her riches. Some versions (RSV, NEB) render verse 8 so that God speaks in its latter part. God answered Israel's boast of riches by saying that no amassed wealth could obscure an awful fact. Her gain had come by oppression of the weak and shady business ethics. Many interpreters prefer this reading because it provides a smooth movement to Jehovah's decree in the next verse.

Was the statement that the people once more would "dwell in tents" (v. 9) a threat or promise? We cannot be certain. Before making the statement, God spoke again of his individuality and power to redeem. The feast referred to was Tabernacles, which was a time of special thanksgiving for God's miraculous guidance and tender mercies for the past year. It was a joyous affair, coming only five days after the mournful Day of Atonement. This forecast, however, seems to be a threat, not a promise. God would not turn from his earnest intent to redeem the world through Israel. The people must, however, learn discipline. They must be brought once again to the type of living endured during the forty years from Egypt to Canaan. Thus they would come to know their need for the Lord. A gleam of promise may be present, however. A small amount of food would be available, even though the people were forced to abide in the booths (tents) of austere living.

The prophets were God's special gift to Israel. They appeared under many guises. Often their messages were in parables or symbols, but their basic truth was always the same. Their ecstatic visions were rooted in moral and ethical truth. Israel, however, had remained deaf to their pleadings. Ruin was sure, and no one but Israel was to blame.

Gilead and Gilgal represented the two major sections of the Northern Kingdom. Gilead stood for the land east of the Jordan River, and Gilgal the west. Both were religious centers and had become strongholds of idol worship. Most likely, the statement about Gilead and Gilgal is a parallelism. Each had adopted worship forms inconsistent with God's holiness. The sacrificing of bullocks (see Lev. 23:18) was not wrong in itself. It was condemned because it was done as a part of pagan worship. The gifts were dedicated to the Canaanite gods rather than Jehovah. Also the rites were corrupt and an outrage to the holy nature of Israel's God.

Some students translate verse 11 "their altars shall become heaps." This translation makes the clause refer to the land's future pillage. The Hebrew allows the clause to be so rendered, but does not demand it. The clause could be translated "their altars are as heaps in the furrows of the field." Hosea could have been referring to the large number of worship places. On the other hand, a play on words may be present. Gilgal was called Heap-town because of its meaning in the Hebrew. One translator renders this clause "droppings of animals to be found in the furrows which they had plowed."

No real point of doctrine is involved. The prophet could have described a state that was present or future. The threat can be left out in verse 11 and not soften the prophet's message. He clearly foretold utter ruin for the nation in verse 14 of this section.

In verse 12 Hosea returned to the life of Jacob. He told how the patriarch fled to Syria and worked hard to secure his wife. We cannot be certain of Hosea's purpose in his reference to this story. God blessed Jacob in spite of his crafty actions. He was brought back to his father's house in peace. The next verse (13) may explain verse 12. The people had come to depend upon God's promise to Abraham for their claim to the land. Hosea pointed out that they were a redeemed people. Through Moses they had been brought from Egypt. Also God had given witness of himself through the years by prophets who had declared his purpose for the nation. Israel would be blessed if she obeyed him.

One phase of Jehovah's holy nature is his righteous anger. He shows intense favor for everything that is good. He must, however, oppose that which is impure and bad. In verse 14 Hosea made plain Israel's ingratitude and rebellion against God. God had no option; he had to oppose Israel's sin. Verse 14, which pictures God as leaving Ephraim to suffer sin's effects, suggests also how God judges. God permits sin to run its course. Israel's sin must be borne by the guilty nation. Because God is consistent, Israel would reap what she had sown. (See Gal. 6:7-9.)

4. Sin's Vicious Circle *(13:1-3)*

Whether chapter 13 stands by itself or is a part of the larger section, one fact is certain. We have come to the final statement of Israel's doom. In fact, this chapter sums up all that has gone before. Hosea spoke of the Lord's tender care of Israel during the early years. He pointed out Israel's forgetfulness and moral decline. The weakness of the kings and stupidity of the people had led to national disaster (vv. 5-6). The chapter closes with a horrible picture of the enemy's almost unbelievable cruelty and the nation's awful fate (vv. 15-16).

The first three verses describe the past, present, and future in one quick summary. The phrase concerning Ephraim's speaking and trembling (13:1) has been rendered a number of ways. A quick glance at several modern versions reveals the many translations. The best approach, most likely, is that which pictures Ephraim as speaking and the others as trembling. In most of Hosea's oracles, Ephraim is the same as Israel, the Northern Kingdom. Here, however, Hosea spoke of the tribe named for one of Joseph's sons.

In the early years Ephraim was one of the most respected of the twelve tribes. She was looked to as a leader and was, in fact, the largest of the group. Pride, however, led Ephraim to sin. At the rupture of the unified kingdom in 931 B.C., Ephraim was among those who embraced a form of Baal worship as a means for maintaining unity in the Northern Kingdom. (See 1 Kings 12:25-33.) Later, under Ahab and Jezebel, a new and even more God-dishonoring type of pagan worship flowed in from Phoenicia. (See 1 Kings 16:29-33.) In Hosea's day this idol worship permeated the entire land.

The idols which the people had made "according to their own understanding" (v. 2) represented the works of their hands. Any society faces danger when it proudly looks to its own wisdom rather than to the truths that come from the worship of the true God. Many sins begin with the feeling that we have a knowledge above our Creator's.

The latter part of verse 2 has been brought from Hebrew into English in various ways. Some versions render it as though human sacrifice had become a part of Israel's normal worship rites. This rendering is doubtful, although events of this nature occurred later in Judah. (See 2 Kings 16:3; 17:17.) Those who brought sacrifices kissed the calves as part of the religious rites. Hosea's statement was ironic and bristles with sarcasm.

Four figures of speech are used in verse 3 to picture the coming ruin. They all convey urgency. The first two, morning cloud and early dew, are symbols of that which is in itself good, but passing. The other two, chaff and smoke, picture that which is worthless from the start. Israel did indeed begin with great promise, but her goodness dissolved and was as if it had never been. The chaff lay on the floor with the wheat. The owner threw both into the air. The wind blew the chaff away, and the wheat fell back to the floor. What a marvelously accurate picture of the coming judgment! From time to time the prophets promised that a remnant would survive. They would become the nucleus for God's redemptive work in the future. The smoke was a picture of Ephraim's prosperity. Unsolid and greatly inflated, it swelled, ascended, and vanished into the air. The four pictures combine to show Israel's guilt, lack of power, and the coming judgment. God through Hosea had decreed as a certain fact that Israel could not escape.

5. Israel's Ingratitude and Doom (*13:4-8*)

This poem has two sections. In verses 4-6 God brought his charge against the nation. In verses 7-8 he pronounced his verdict. Israel was a redeemed people. Jehovah, the Self-existing One, had brought her from Egypt. He was not merely her God and Savior; he was her only Savior. God reserved for himself complete claim to be Israel's Redeemer. He would share that distinction with no one.

God's tender care of Israel during the forty years she wandered was clear proof of his love and concern for her. The verb "know" is one of the most intimate to be found in the Old Testament. Hosea used it in verse 4 to picture the people's closeness to God. In that context it means "to experience the benefits and presence of another." In verse 5 it is used of God's gracious act toward the people. Some versions render it "pastored." In the latter context Hosea used it in much the same way as Amos 3:2, where the idea of approval or a special blessing is present. During the time they wandered, the nation had to depend upon Jehovah alone. Had it not been for his grace, they would have perished shortly after leaving Egypt.

How could people so blessed have turned away from the One who was responsible for their well-being? Yet this is what happened. Quoting Moses almost word for word (Deut. 8:12,14), Hosea warned the people against failing to remain grateful when they prospered (v. 6).

This section begins with a picture of God as the nation's protector and ends with him as destroyer. The change had come because of Israel's disloyalty. The shepherd of the flock must now turn upon her in judgment. The figure of three wild beasts is used to convey the message: a hungry lioness, a crouching leopard, and an enraged she bear whose cubs have been killed. The expression "rend the caul of their heart" (v. 8) most likely refers to the attack of the lioness, which goes instinctively to the heart of her prey, tears it out, and sucks the blood.

This shocking, but true, picture depicts the actual events that occurred at the downfall of Israel. In 734 B.C. the Syrians depopulated most of both Gilead and Galilee. In 725 B.C. a siege was thrown around the capital, Samaria. This blockade lasted for three years. In 722 B.C. the capital fell. By 721 B.C. almost all the people had been carried into exile. Although these verbs denote future action, the first of them may describe action already in progress. For this reason many versions render the opening statement, "I have become unto them" (v. 7), thus showing the punishment as having begun. This reading is in keeping with the date these words likely were uttered by the prophet.

6. Israel's Inability to Understand the Crisis (*13:9-11*)

A new train of thought begins with verse 9. Hosea's concise sayings may have shades of meaning. Actually, five Hebrew words occur in the verse. Literally they read, "It has destroyed thee, Israel, because against me against thy help." Bible interpreters have sought to smooth out the Hebrew in an English translation. The main point, however, is clear. Israel was her own worst enemy. The nation's ruin had come about because the people had refused their only source of strength. Norman Snaith has expressed the passage's meaning clearly: "There is no thing, no person, no institution, no book, no anything at all, except only God, whom we can trust. There is nothing at all which can be to any degree a substitute for the living God, who is to be known in the experience of trusting Him day by day and relying upon Him continually." [2] Israel had refused to find her help in the living God. She had revolted and in so doing had signed her own death warrant.

To be certain about Hosea's feeling toward the kingship is difficult. He may have disliked, as Samuel did, the very idea. Whatever view he took, we know he saw how weak Israel's rulers had become. He knew they were not able to meet Israel's crisis. During the last years of her life the nation's kings fared badly. Only one of her last six kings died a natural death. The nation clung to a belief that the right king could and would save her. An irony of history is that Israel's last king bore the proud name "Hoshea," which means "salvation" or "deliverance." None of her kings was able to deliver Israel.

Verse 11 shows that God gave Israel a king in his anger and took him away in his wrath. This reference may be to the setting up of the kingship in the days of Samuel (1 Sam. 8:7) and the final ruin of the nation in 722 B.C. More than likely, however, the verbs express repeated action. Thus the Lord acted on more than one occasion and was still acting in Hosea's day. During the 209 years of the Northern Kingdom's existence (931-722 B.C.), Israel's kings often were killed, and new royal houses set up. The Northern Kingdom itself was set up in rebellion against Solomon's true heir. Were all of these things done with or without the Lord's permission? Did the people act upon their own impulses? In the ultimate sense both implied charges are true. Paul made clear in Romans that often God gives people up to their own sins. (See Rom. 1:28-32.) Although the Lord was not consulted, none of these changes could have come about without his consent. In one sense, the people made the kings; in another, the Lord gave them. In every case the Lord took them away. The confusion, chaos, and anarchy which followed each royal death were due to God's judgment upon sin.

7. Dying by Refusing to Live (*13:12-13*)

When we refuse to repent of sin, our guilt deepens. Hosea insisted that the people not hold the false notion that God would ignore their sins. Hosea believed the sins were in heaven's record. The guilt would not fade with the passing of time. Like legal documents stored up for future use, Israel's sins were "bound up" (v. 12) to await the day of judgment. Hosea's heart must have broken as he set forth this harsh message about Israel's fate. A sensitive person, he found warning the people he loved difficult. Yet he had to speak thus because the evidence was in the divine record. The ledger was about to be added up, and the sum of the nation's sins set forth clearly. Judgment was coming.

In verse 13 Hosea used the picture of a woman in labor. She was not able to bring forth her child and thus bring an end to the pain and suffering. A double thrust to the nation's problem is present. First, the actual childbirth pain and distress is unavoidable. Likewise Israel must experience violent and overwhelming pain when God chastises her.

An even more profound truth is present in this metaphor. Israel is a child that will not emerge from the womb in spite of the mother's labor pains. This condition meant acute crisis. Two lives were in danger—the mother's and the child's. The truth to Israel was that the nation even at this last hour could have new birth. A new spirit and a secure future were Israel's if she would accept the life which the Lord offered. If she refused God's grace, she would be as a child lingering in the womb. If the sin-sick nation remained on her present course, both the people of the land and the nation as a whole would die a violent death. To remain rebellious was folly. If Israel stayed stubborn and would not enter into a new life, she would plunge from the threshold of destruction into the abyss of complete collapse.

8. A Threat or a Promise? (*13:14*)

The substance of this verse was quoted by Paul (1 Cor. 15:55). (Present also in the Pauline verse is a clause from Isa. 25:8.) Paul presented a profound truth, but in the form of several questions. Those questions imply that that which can be corrupted on earth also can be changed. The mortal can give way to immortality. There is no doubt concerning Paul's use of the verse. All readers, however, do not agree on the meaning within the context of Hosea's message.

First are those who contend that this verse is a threat. They believe the first two clauses should be viewed as rhetorical questions, or at least viewed as questions which expect a negative answer. Therefore God would not ransom Israel from the power of the grave or redeem her from death. The next two clauses, addressed to death and the grave, challenge them to do their worst to Israel. God had turned the nation over to be destroyed by them. In the final clause the word "repentance" should be rendered "compassion" (v. 14). This verse conveys the thought that God would show no mercy at all to the condemned nation. Verses 15-16 then expand this threat.

Other interpreters insist this verse is an example of Hosea's lingering hopes and promises extended to the condemned people. Although he always faced facts as to Israel's doom, Hosea also had hope for the future. Since Paul used this verse to picture coming joy when the dead bodies of those in Christ would be raised (1 Cor. 15:55), this view has some support. To accept this verse as promise rather than as threat ties in with what we know of God's nature. Although the flouting of God's love calls forth his judgment, God's love is stronger than judgment. Thus Israel's judgment would not end the unique relationship between her and God. He would still bring to pass his proposal to redeem the world through Israel. God would use his own unlimited resources to accomplish his purpose.

9. A Final Picture of Coming Calamity (*13:15-16*)

Hosea's figure of a torrid wind from the eastern desert (v. 15) represents Assyria. She was chosen by God to do his avenging work. The land would be laid waste and turned into a barren desert. The phrase "treasure of all goodly vessels" (v. 15) refers to the wealth of the land. When the enemy came, the people would be reduced to poverty.

The last verse of this section is one of the harshest and most shocking to be found in the book. Hosea mentioned "Samaria" (v. 16) because it was the capital of the land. All areas of life in the royal city had been corrupt. God would make a striking example of it. Hosea used the picture of war to describe the judgment. This picture shows what war was like then as well as now.

10. Lessons for Life from the Scriptures

The prophet's picture of Israel's tragic end has a message for our day. No nation can ignore the built-in moral and spiritual structures of the universe. We cannot sin without being punished. This section has an urgent message for us today.

Unstable people fly to any source for help. Some people seem not able to remain loyal to any cause or person for a long time. They change friends, jobs, churches—never finding lasting peace. The problem is within the person, not outside. Some people seem unable to build relationships. Sometimes they adopt strange behavior patterns. Although they have emotional problems, they also have deep spiritual problems. Indeed the latter are more likely the cause of the former.

Unholy gain will never endure. When one forfeits principles for wealth, he is sowing the seed for future distress. True wealth is the success that comes in life because one has trusted God. Such a person will follow God in grateful living and with a humble spirit. The tenure of worldly wealth is short. Power, stability, true riches, and joy are found in God alone. When we oppress others, practice deceit, or defend injustice to amass riches, we are building on sand. There will be no shelter of security when the time of testing comes.

The sinner is his own worst enemy. The lack of spiritual power can often be traced to the failure of moral self-control. The sinner has no one to blame but himself. Circumstances do not force a person to sin. Neither does fate compel him to make wrong choices. The guilt lies upon the sinner's head. He faces death because he wills to die rather than live.

With God there is always hope. Although man may be bent on destroying himself, God still saves to the uttermost. Even at the midnight hour the door is open for those who will accept the full, free, and universal invitation of divine mercy. In Jesus Christ, God has destroyed the power of death. The Savior's triumph becomes our victory when we receive him in faith. God's people are free. They may live without fear of death. The weakest believer can confront his most deadly foe with an assurance of triumph through Christ.

---

[1] Joseph Addison Alexander, "The Hidden Line," in *A Quest for Souls,* by George W. Truett (Dallas: Texas Baptist Book House, 1917), pp. 370-71.

[2] Norman H. Snaith, *Amos, Hosea and Micah* (London: The Epworth Press, n.d.), p. 81.

PERSONAL LEARNING ACTIVITIES

1. Match the Scripture phrase (KJV) as found in Hosea 11:12 to 13:16 with the Scripture reference and the meaning:

___ ___"The east wind"	(1) 12:8	(a) Israel's instability
___ ___"The Lord . . . will punish Jacob"	(2) 12:2	(b) Israel's boast
___ ___"Yet I am become rich"	(3) 12:1	(c) Israel likened to Jacob
___ ___"Morning cloud . . . dew . . . chaff . . . smoke"	(4) 13:7,8	(d) Figures to describe God's judgment on Israel's sin
___ ___"Lion . . . leopard . . . bear"	(5) 13:3	(e) Israel's behavior

---

Answers:

1. (3),(e); (2),(c); (1),(b); (5),(a); (4),(d).

10
A Future for Failures

HOSEA 14:1-9

A prophet of God cannot compromise his moral integrity. He must condemn sin and proclaim judgment. Israel's inner corruption had made necessary Hosea's expression of shocking disgust with the nation's conduct. He did not shirk his duty. While sin sapped the strength and glory of the nation, the prophet was spelling out in unmistakable ways the nation's fate. Israel was like a house whose timbers, eaten by termites, had become empty shells. Sudden collapse was not only sure; it was on its way. Few prophets ever pointed out a nation's problem more clearly than Hosea did.

There is, however, another side to prophetic preaching. A man of God must perceive that underlying every threat of divine judgment is a summons to repentance and a call to mercy. Man has a free will; so does God. Regardless of how clearly Hosea had described the coming judgment, the sentence could be commuted if the people would turn to God in heartfelt repentance.

Hosea's feelings were keen because of his tragedy at home. He had learned the pain of loving. Having known the anguish of forgiving a straying wife, he could grasp God's feeling toward Israel. Hosea had been lonely. This dark valley had equipped him to understand God's longing for companionship with the nation that had forsaken him. After being stretched upon the rack of tortured love, Hosea knew God's anguish. Hosea had gone on loving Gomer in spite of her wayward conduct and desertion. He knew from his own experience that God would not desert Israel.

This last chapter has three sections. The first (vv. 1-3) contains a plea for the people to repent. Hosea begged them to return to their God (v. 1). In verses 2-3 he put words of repentance into the mouths of the people. The second section (vv. 4-8) contains words of Jehovah. Over the stormy waters of judgment he threw a rainbow of hope. The prophet's splendid pictures remind us of the Song of Solomon. If only the people would accept God's gracious pardon promised in his loving wooing, Israel could know future blessings. The third section (v. 9) is an epilogue to the entire book. The wisdom set forth by the prophet is praised. Those who rebelled and refused would learn that the way of the transgressor is hard.

This grand call to repentance, followed by promise of pardon, ends the book ideally. Some students, however, do not believe it was Hosea's last message to the people. To them, the final doom in chapter 13 was too definite. They believe this gracious call came earlier, when there was hope the people would avoid the doom to which they were rushing. But the date the words were spoken does not affect the truth and spiritual worth of the passage. The mingling of mercy and judgment was a unique trait of Hosea's. We are on solid ground in taking this as his last sermon. Hosea was bringing love's final appeal to a people standing on the brink of extinction. Even though the previous threat had seemed final, it was not his last word. Hosea could not end his ministry on this note. He must make one more attempt to bring his people back to the heart of their loving Father.

1. A Call to Repentance (*14:1*)

Hosea had keen insight into human weakness. Israel's crisis was more than a cosmic roller coaster ride to ruin. The people were not in the hands of a cruel fate, nor had God harshly assigned them to a headlong fall over the precipice. Their plight was the result of their sin.

Only one solution was offered. Israel must repent. If the people refused to make a choice, their future was political ruin, perhaps extinction. The time had come for Israel to face the issue. Hosea was not sent to announce doom. His work was that of bringing the people back to God. Even God, however, could not save people who wished to remain in bondage and be enslaved by passions of their own lower nature.

The word "return" (v. 1) is used often in the Old Testament for the turning which comes when one truly repents. The Hebrew word means "to turn about, turn back, or return." This may be a return to a person or to a thing. Also the word may mean the return of an article to a former owner. A derived idea is that of conversion. When "return" is used in the sense of returning to God, the idea of sorrow for sin committed is present. This leads to the concept of repentance. This Hebrew idea is forerunner to the New Testament teaching on repentance leading to salvation.

The need for the command is set forth clearly. The nation was without excuse for its sin and without power in its own strength to rise above it. The word "fallen" (v. 1) means "stumble" or "to be visited by a calamity." Hosea thus spoke of the coming ruin as though it had begun to take place. The word "iniquity" (v. 1) has a double thrust. It means "moral crookedness" or "perversity." Also the idea of guilt because of crooked deeds is part of the word's meaning. No other way to remain useful in God's plan was present. The nation must change its present course and come back to God. The people must come all the way back, not just part of the way.

Two words in verse 1 should be noted. First, Hosea addressed the nation as Israel. This name was used most often for the ten tribes. Hosea conveyed a vital truth. The prophet included all the people left in what has been called the Northern Kingdom. He might have meant even those who had been taken captive in a campaign before 722 B.C. Also the message applies only to the Northern Kingdom. Although Hosea sometimes had words for Judah, this message was to Israel alone.

The second word to note is the expression "Jehovah thy God." The first proper noun was the unique name by which God had revealed himself to the nation. Its meaning is that God *is* always. He has existed, he exists, and he shall continue to exist. Also he is the unique, self-revealed God of the Israelites. He made a promise to Abram long before the law was given at Sinai. He chose Israel to be the means by which his plan would come to pass. God made Israel in a unique sense for himself.

2. A Suggested Prayer for the Nation (*14:2-3*)

A command heard often was, "None shall appear before me empty" (Ex. 23:15; 34:20). Costly gifts brought to regain the Lord's favor were not enough for this crisis. The people had lavished silver and gold on their idols. God wanted no part of this approach.

At first reading, one may see the command, "Take with you words," as something without much meaning. Roy Honeycutt, however, shows deep insight into the meaning of this command. He says: "No one should assume that God can be coerced or cajoled into the renewal of fellowship. God does not need Israel's words, but Israel desperately needs to articulate in specifics her petition as well as her contrition and commitment." [1]

The rest of verse 2 and all of verse 3 contain Israel's prayer. This was the means of Israel's access to God. This prayer, voiced by Hosea for the people, may have become a regular part of the Temple service. When the hot breath of Babylon blew upon Judah, wise men saw the time was short. Hosea must have been quoted often then. Judah's last prophet, Jeremiah, showed clearly his knowledge of Hosea's messages.

In the Hebrew text the word "all" comes first in verse 2. This gives a strong force to the need for Israel's thorough confession of her sin. The Hebrew word "forgive" is translated "take away." The word pictures a lifting up and carrying off. It is used often in the Old Testament for forgiveness. The prophet was not asking God to accept sacrifices. Israel had done an overkill on ritual. The Hebrew phrase "take good" (v. 2, translated "accept that which is good") may have one of two meanings. First is the idea that the Lord is to take and use that which is good—his mercy. In this way he will receive the people once more into his favor. The other and preferred meaning is that Israel was asking God to accept the only good they could offer—prayer and repentance.

The last phrase in verse 2 is not easy to translate. The Hebrew says, "We will render bullocks' lips." Most translators render it smoothly, making Hosea say that Israel would bring words of repentance and confession, not costly gifts. R. F. Horton says, "Words take the place of formal offerings, therefore lips take the place of her costly bullocks that were offered." [2]

The reference to Assyria is clear. Israel will no longer put her trust in foreign treaties with strong nations. This practice, which both Hosea and Isaiah had condemned, will be laid aside. The nation will return to God as her source of stength. The way will be paved then for future Israel to be once more a nation whose king is Jehovah.

The reference to horses in verse 3 may have two possible meanings. First, horses were the symbol for military strength. Solomon took pride in his stables, and viewed them as proof of the nation's strength in battle. These prized resources were condemned by the prophets. Hezekiah, one of Judah's best kings, refrained from building large stables. He probably felt to do so would have shown a lack of trust in God. The Assyrian Rabshakeh taunted Isaiah when Jerusalem was besieged. He said, "I will give thee two thousand horses, if thou be able on thy part to set riders upon them" (Isa. 36:8).

A second meaning may be in the fact that Solomon and his successors received their horses from Egypt. Thus Hosea's word about horses may parallel his statement about Assyria. In other words, he conveyed the idea the people must cease to depend upon any foreign power, Assyria or Egypt. The first was mentioned by name, and the other implied.

The phrase "work of our hands" (v. 3) clearly refers to idol worship. Whatever else may be said of the Jewish people in post-Exilic days, one thing is clear. The Exile purged Israel of any dealing with idols. The Jews came forth from Babylon believing in one God, and they have remained faithful to this concept ever since. The Jews have never gone back to idol worship like that practiced before the two kingdoms fell.

The last phrase of verse 3 pictures Israel as a helpless orphan. Lonely, she can find aid only in God, who delights in showing mercy to the weak. This image climaxes Israel's repentance and confession. She throws herself utterly upon the grace of the God against whom she has sinned. Israel has no merit. Any favor shown to her will be because her God is infinite in mercy. True conversion and salvation will come only when God's people plead for mercy.

3. God's Forgiving Love (*14:4*)

Starting with verse 4, the prophet spoke *about* Israel, rather than *to* her. Also he identified himself with God and spoke in the first person as though God himself were making the statements. The phrase "I will" is used three times in this verse and the next. God will heal her backsliding, love her freely, and be as the dew unto her.

Because of what he suffered, Hosea believed in the therapy of love. He compared the people's state to a disease which required the treatment of a doctor. When the people were willing to repent, God was quick to respond. Two truths are present in God's promise to "heal their backsliding" (v. 4). First, he would remove the guilt of their sin. In doing so, he would deal with the cause of the calamity which had come upon them. Their present hopeless condition was because of their rebellious spirit. The very essence of forgiveness is its personal nature. Sin is not a thing apart from the sinner. It is involved in his own relationship to God and in his response to God's way of life for him. Therefore, to forgive means to reconcile and to transform. In no sense can it be considered merely a prelude to anything.

The verse which follows (v. 5) shows how God heals the damage caused by sin. Covering up the damage may be our main concern, but not God's. He seeks the inner change that comes through the working of his Spirit. The New Testament calls this change regeneration, or the new birth. God's glorious grace does cover our sin. We should note, however, that God does not remove the temporal consequences of past sin. To do so would disturb the normal operation of our moral and physical order. We reap in our bodies and relationships what we sow (Gal. 6:7-8).

God's love is self-acting. We are not required to bring him a freewill offering in order to secure his favor. His love cannot be purchased. God asks repentance and the resolve to follow a new life course. This act must be sincere and must lead one to adopt a new set of values in daily living.

Hosea spoke of God's anger as being "turned away" (v. 4). God's anger was righteous indignation toward the nation's sin. The New Testament concept of God's wrath is the divine reaction to sin, not personal revenge. Hosea's concept was very much the same; he was just much more dramatic. In verse 4 the prophet changed pronouns in dealing with Israel. At first, he spoke of *them,* and then at the last, he narrowed his message to *him.* This was no accident of language, nor error of grammar. The prophet wrote thus on purpose as a part of his unique style. He was seeking to make his message intensely personal.

4. God's Life-Giving Power (*14:5*)

When two estranged people become reconciled, many new thoughts and actions emerge. No one figure of speech can exhaust God's resources. He has power both to provide for the needs of his people and enrich their lives. Hosea was a poet as well as a prophet. His picture of Israel's future was expressed in language which had special meaning to the people of that geographical area. Dew meant much during the entire year, but was urgently needed during the drought from May until October. Dew became a vivid symbol for that which refreshed and brought vigor. Twice before, Hosea had used this figure, but with a different meaning. The first time (6:4), dew was used to describe the people's shallow goodness. The second (13:3), it was used as a symbol of judgment. Here, however, it has a new meaning. The promise was that the Lord would put new energy and life into his people.

This figure of speech, "the dew," is rich. Dew falls quietly upon the grass. Likewise God comes in stillness. Dew comes in darkness when the sun has set, when the breath of evening has come, and the curtain of night has been drawn. Also God helps us in the dark moments of our lives. Another beautiful truth emerges. Did you know dew is always heaviest upon the lowest ground? We do not find much of it on the tops of mountains. Likewise God comes most often and is received most readily by the humble.

Switching to the figure of a lily, Hosea stressed another aspect of the Lord's blessing. Beauty as well as stateliness is set forth. Also present is the idea of fertility and rapid multiplication. One ancient writer says that the lily cannot be equaled in its volume of reproduction. One single root often produces as many as fifty bulbs. People were important to a small kingdom hemmed in by hostile nations. Numbers meant large work crews and military strength. The "roots as Lebanon" (v. 5) may refer either to the great cedars or the imposing mountain. The book of Job (28:9) speaks of mountains as having roots. Either image suggests something stable, but the concept of Israel's being like the great mountain is striking. George Adam Smith speaks of how Lebanon dominates all of this land. He refers to the snow peak which gathers the clouds and discovers the streams, rests the eyes of weary travelers in the unwholesome plain, and lifts up the hearts of pilgrims to the heavens. To be therefore like the deep-rooted, steadfast, far seen, and much-loved mountain was better than to be like the fairest of its flowers and the stateliest of its trees.[3] Israel would grow fast like the lily. Also she would have permanence like the great range of mountains in Lebanon and its giant trees.

5. Israel's Growing Influence *(14:6-7)*

Israel's past had not been a thing of beauty. Her future, however, would be filled with glory. No longer weak and yielding to every temptation, she would grow in strength. Rather than staying as a withered and dying bush in the desert, she would be filled with vigor. As a thriving plant she would spread her roots farther and farther. Israel would be more than a tree. She would become a complete garden. The word "branches" (v. 6) refers to the tender shoots which have not yet matured. Hosea was not mixing metaphors loosely. He rather blended figures of speech to present the complete picture of the restored and renewed Israel. The lily is beautiful, but has no strong roots. Both mountains and cedars of Lebanon have deep roots. Hosea combined the spreading branches with the beauty of the olive tree and the fragrance of the Lebanon cedars. The old Israel had failed, but a new Israel would arise. All the ideals God had cherished for his people would be realized in this new Israel. The old was ugly, impure, deformed, weak, and unstable. The new would be noted for its beauty, purity, strength, and fidelity. The highest and the noblest were in the future for God's reconciled and restored people.

In verse 7 the Lord is still the speaker. The expression "his shadow" refers to Israel. Individuals of the nation would come to live in harmony with God's principles. As a result, they would prosper. The revived grain, the blooming vine, and the fragrant scent all are related to Israel's renewal and increase. Corn dies and then multiplies. Branches on a vine must be pruned in order to bear richer fruit. Grapes must be crushed to produce wine. Likewise Israel must suffer through the heavy hand of chastisement. Only in this way could God make her pure. After God's work had been done, Israel would bear abundant fruits of grace. Israel had failed God, but his mercy would not give her up. The nation, once a luxuriant but empty vine, could be changed. Israel still would become rich in vitality, prolific in fruit bearing, and fragrant in odor. Her goodness, however, must not be fleeting, but abiding. Man cannot sin without being punished. But through God's mercy he can repent and be saved. God still invited man to his salvation even until the last moment. Hosea used all the resources of language at his command. He sought to make the people see their beautiful future in right relationship to God.

6. Israel's Needs Completely Satisfied (*14:8*)

The Lord's last word to his forgiven and restored people is viewed by some interpreters as a dialogue between Ephraim and Jehovah. Most likely, however, Hosea spoke for God throughout the entire verse. Some translators insert "shall say" after the first word to smooth out the translation. The best reading is the Revised Standard Version which reads, "O Ephraim, what have I to do with idols?" God looked at the nation and saw there were no strange gods in the land. He knew he could supply the needs of his people. He therefore made it abundantly clear that he deserved their wholehearted service. The implied answer to the question is that God has nothing to do with idols. Since the nation had forsaken them, he could be to them a never failing source of blessing.

To know the exact type of tree Hosea had in mind in verse 8 is difficult. The "green fir-tree" was most likely a leafy cypress. He likely was thinking of the splendid cypress trees of Mount Lebanon. Even as the branches of this stately tree swept out and down toward the earth, so God would reach down from heaven to care for Israel's needs. God is unchangeable in his concern for his people's welfare. He would both protect them and shelter them forever.

Has this chapter been fulfilled? The reader is referred to the author's comments concerning 1:10 to 2:1 in an earlier chapter. Christendom is divided as to the future of national Israel. Some Christians believe passages such as this one await fulfillment in a literal sense. Others believe spiritual Israel has absorbed the promises made to national Israel (Rom. 2:28-29; Gal. 3:29). One thing is certain. The God of Hosea's day is our God also. He has been revealed clearly in Jesus Christ. His demands for righteous living and his fervent love are still with us. They are as real and relevant today as they were when the brokenhearted prophet pleaded with Israel to return to God and be healed.

7. An Epilogue—Wisdom of Those Heeding (*14:9*)

In verse 9 the words "wise" and "prudent" are not synonyms. In the Hebrew the first word means "intelligent." The second word means "acting according to this knowledge." The prudent person squares the way he acts with the way he knows is right. The two verbs "understand" and "know" also present a contrast. The first speaks of insight, while the second relates to experience. This plea for wisdom in action is a worthy climax to Hosea's series of messages. He combined stern judgment and merciful love. Thus the last word was a plea for Israel to translate into daily living the truths trumpeted by the prophet.

The last statement is a brief of the wisdom literature of an earlier period. Sin carries with it the seed of its own destruction. Man lives in a moral universe in which God governs through righteous laws. Wisdom is more than formal training or content knowledge. It involves one's gaining insight in order to grasp moral reality. By seeking, finding, and obeying the eternal truths of God, man enjoys fulfillment.

The God who redeems us purposes that we walk in his statutes free from guilt, but also free from deceit, guile, and willful sin. Through Hosea's closing warning, God makes his appeal to us.

8. Lessons for Life from the Scriptures

Sin makes salvation necessary. God created man in perfect fellowship with himself. Eden's tragedy was man's rebellion against God, the rupture of his relationship with God. What a painful loss it was! Sin does more than make man unfit for communion with God. Because of sin, man loses the desire for fellowship with God. Man severed from God must be restored to him. Sin made Christ's death on the cross a necessity.

God loves us, but we must repent to be saved. Much preaching today stresses faith in Christ, but says little about repentance. A changed life comes because of repentance. Through it God's Holy Spirit is able to perform a life-changing work in the heart.

Human resources are not sufficient. One of our most serious mistakes today is to think we can meet life's needs in our own strength. To be sure, man should use his own knowledge. Doing so is good common sense. Wise people, however, are not deceived. They know only Jesus Christ can bring peace. He does that through his reconciling love, which produces peace.

Forgiven people have unlimited potential. The knowledge that one's sins have been forgiven tends toward mental health. Guilt is gone because God in Jesus Christ has borne that guilt. When one receives Jesus as personal Savior, he can realize the fruit of the Spirit in his life (see Gal. 5:22-23). Love, unselfishness, compassion, and all the other virtues prompted by the Spirit become a part of his life. The estimate of the glorious things which may be done with such a life is boundless. The future of redeemed failures is unlimited.

Life with God is beautiful. When one has given himself to the Savior's way of life, he adopts a new set of values. No longer is he living for the lust of the moment. Rather, he is taking a long-range view of life. This means, among other things, he is feeding his soul with God's lovely words—righteousness, mercy, and peace. Guarding his life closely, he seeks to forbid the entrance of anything that would subvert God's holy will. Such a life is both rich within and lovely without.

Wise people listen to God's Word. Although God speaks in many ways, the Bible for us is the supreme record of what God has revealed. In it we find wisdom for living and authority for action.

---

[1] Honeycutt, *op. cit.*, p. 59.

[2] R. F. Horton, ed., *The Century Bible*, Minor Prophets, Vol. 1 (Edinburgh: T.C. & E.C. Jack, n.d.), p. 73.

[3] Smith, *op. cit.*, pp. 341,344.

PERSONAL LEARNING ACTIVITIES

1. The author states that Hosea 14 has three parts. From the following list identify those parts and their proper sequence:
   (1) Hosea's plea to the people to repent
   (2) The people's rejection of the prophet's plea

(3) An epilogue to the book
(4) God's words to Israel

2. The word "return" in Hosea 14:1 means (check appropriate responses):
   (1) To go back from where one has come
   (2) Repent
   (3) To leave one's present place (either spiritually or physically)
3. Hosea 14:4-9 presents (check correct response):
   (1) Israel's future
   (2) Israel's future if she repents
   (3) A symbolic description of God's new Israel in Christ

Answers:
1. (1), (4), (3); 2. (1), (2), (3); 3. The answer depends upon the reader's interpretation of biblical prophecy as it relates to Israel.

THE CHURCH STUDY COURSE

The Church Study Course consists of a variety of short-term credit courses for adults and youth and noncredit foundational units for children and preschoolers. The materials are for use in addition to the study and training curriculums made available to the churches on an ongoing basis.

Study courses and foundational units are organized into a system that is promoted by the Sunday School Board, 127 Ninth Avenue, North, Nashville, Tennessee 37234, through the departments in the Church Services and Materials Division; by the Woman's Missionary Union, 600 North Twentieth Street, Birmingham, Alabama 35203; by the Brotherhood Commission, 1548 Poplar Avenue, Memphis, Tennessee 38104; and by the respective departments of the state conventions affiliated with the Southern Baptist Convention.

Study course materials are flexible enough to be adapted to the needs of any Baptist church. The resources are published in several different formats—textbooks of various sizes, workbooks, and kits. Each item contains a brief explanation of the Church Study Course and information on requesting credit. Additional information and interpretation are available from the participating agencies.

Types of Study and Credit

Adults and youth can earn study course credit through individual or group study. Youth may take adult courses for credit, but adults can receive credit for youth courses only by teaching them to youth. Teachers of courses or of foundational units are eligible to receive credit.

1. Class Experience.—Group involvement with course material for the designated number of hours for the particular course. A person who is absent from one or more sessions must complete the "Personal Learning Activities" or other requirements for the material missed.
2. Individual Study.—This includes reading, viewing, or listening to course material and completing the specified requirements for the course.
3. Lesson Course Study.—Parallel use of designated study course material during the study of selected units in Church Program Organization periodical curriculum units. Guidance for this means of credit appears in the selected periodical.
4. Institutional Study.—Parallel use of designated study course material during regular courses at educational institutions, including Seminary Extension Department courses. Guidance for this means of credit is provided by the teacher.

Credit is awarded for the successful completion of a course of study. This credit is granted by the Church Study Course Awards Office, 127 Ninth Avenue, North, Nashville, Tennessee 37234, for the participating agencies. Form 151 (available free) is recommended for use in requesting credit.

When credit is issued to a person on request, the Awards Office sends two copies of a notice of credit earned to the church. The original copy of the credit slip should be filed by the study course clerk in the participant's record of training folder. The duplicate should be given to the person who earned the credit. Accumulated credits are applied toward leadership or member development diplomas, which are measures of learning, growth, development, and training.

Detailed information about the Church Study Course system of credits, diplomas, and record keeping is available from the participating agencies. Study course materials, supplementary teaching or learning aids, and forms for record keeping may be ordered from Baptist Book Stores.

The Church Study Course Curriculum

Credit is granted on those courses listed in the current copy of *Church Services and Materials Catalog, Church Study Course Catalog,* and *Baptist Book Store Church Leadership Catalog.* When selecting courses or foundational units, check the current catalogs to determine what course materials are valid.

HOW TO REQUEST CREDIT FOR THIS COURSE

This book is the text for course 3216 of Subject Area 32, Bible Studies.

This course is designed for 5 hours of group study. Credit is awarded for satisfactory class experience with the study material for the minimum number of hours. A person who is absent from one or more sessions must complete the "Personal Learning Activities" or other requirements for the materials missed.

Credit is also allowed for use of this material in individual study and in institutional study, if so designated.

The following requirements must be met for credit in course 3216:

1. Read the book *Hosea: Prophet of Reconciliation.*
2. Attend at least 5 hours of class study or complete all "Personal Learning Activities." A class member who is absent from one or more class sessions must complete "Personal Learning Activities" on chapters missed. In such a case, he must turn in his paper by the date the teacher sets, usually within ten days following the last class.

Credit in course 3216 may be earned through individual study. The requirements for such credit are:

1. Read the book.
2. Complete the "Personal Learning Activities" on the chapters.

Credit in course 3216 may be earned through study in an educational institution, if so designated by a teacher. The requirements are:

1. Read the book.
2. Fulfill the requirements of the course taught at the institution.

After the course is completed, the teacher, the study course clerk, the learner, or any person designated by the church should complete Form 151 ("Request for Course Credit") and send it to the Awards Office, 127 Ninth Avenue, North, Nashville, Tennessee 37234. In this product the reader will find on page 139 a form which he may cut out, fill in, and send to the Awards Office.

Cut along this line

INSTRUCTIONS: If requested by the teacher, fill in this form and give it to him when the course is completed. If preferred, mail this request for course credit to

AWARDS OFFICE
THE SUNDAY SCHOOL BOARD, SBC
127 NINTH AVENUE, NORTH
NASHVILLE, TENNESSEE 37234

Indicate Type of Study (✓)

☐ Individual ☐ Class ☐ Educational Institution Study

State Convention	Association	Church Name

Address of Church (Street, Route, or P.O. Box)	City	State	Zip Code

Mail to: (If Different from Church Address)	Address (Street, Route, or P.O. Box)	City	State	Zip Code

Last Name	First Name	Middle Name	MRS. (X)	COURSE TITLE	COURSE CODE
				Hosea: Prophet of Reconciliation	3216